T0033107

THE
MONTESSORI
BOOK OF
WORDS
AND NUMBERS

THE MONTESSORI BOOK OF WORDS AND NUMBERS

RAISING
A CREATIVE
AND
CONFIDENT
CHILD

MAJA PITAMIC

First published in the USA and Canada in 2022 by Sourcebooks LLC
P.O. Box 4410, Naperville, Illinois 60567-4410
(630) 961-3900
sourcebooks.com

Conceived and produced by
Elwin Street Productions
10 Elwin Street
London E2 7BU

Copyright © Elwin Street Limited 2019

All rights reserved. No part of this book may be reproduced in any form or by any electronic or mechanical means including information storage and retrieval systems—except in the case of brief quotations embodied in critical articles or reviews—without permission in writing from its publisher, Sourcebooks.

This publication is designed to provide accurate and authoritative information in regard to the subject matter covered. It is sold with the understanding that the publisher is not engaged in rendering legal, accounting, or other professional service. If legal advice or other expert assistance is required, the services of a competent professional person should be sought. —From a Declaration of Principles Jointly Adopted by a Committee of the American Bar Association and a Committee of Publishers and Associations

All brand names and product names used in this book are trademarks, registered trademarks, or trade names of their respective holders. Sourcebooks is not associated with any product or vendor in this book.

Some of the text from this book previously appeared in *Teach Me to Do It Myself* (2008).

Illustrations by Isabel Alberdi

ISBN 978-1-4380-8999-7

[Cataloging-in-Publication Data is on file with the Library of Congress]

Printed and bound in the United Arab Emirates.

XX 10 9 8 7 6 5 4 3 2 1

Picture credits
p. 5 Shutterstock by Monkey Business images; p. 6 Shutterstock by Kdonmuang; p. 7 Shutterstock by Liderina; p. 7 Alamy by moodboard / Alamy Stock Photo; p. 8 Shutterstock by wavebreakmedia; p. 11 Shutterstock by wavebreakmedia; pp. 14, 39 Getty Images by Sydney Bourne; p. 14 Shutterstock by Rawpixel.com; pp. 14, 47 Getty Images by Andersen Ross Photography Inc; p. 27 Shutterstock by Phish Photography; p. 41 Keith Waterton; p. 45 Shutterstock by Monkey Business Images; p. 53 Shutterstock by iordani; p. 55 Shutterstock by Joaquin Corbalan P; p. 61 Alamy by MNStudio / Alamy Stock Photo; p. 73 Shutterstock by Monkey Business Images; p. 79 Shutterstock by Liderina; p. 87 Getty Images by Jose Luis Pelaez Inc; p. 88 Shutterstock by Dragon Images; pp. 88, 92 Keith Waterton; pp. 88, 101 Shutterstock by Kdonmuang; p. 91 Alamy by 2light/ Alamy Stock Photo; p. 111 Getty Images by Hero Images; p. 123 Shutterstock by MNStudio; p. 127 Shutterstock by Joaquin Corbalan P; p. 149 Shutterstock by riekephotos; p. 159 Ellie Smith; p. 165 Alamy by IZA STOCK / Alamy Stock Photo

CONTENTS

1: Word Play

2: Fun with Numbers

ABOUT MONTESSORI

Maria Montessori was born in Rome in 1870 and became the first female medical graduate of Rome University. In 1907, Montessori opened the first Casa dei Bambini, a school for children from slums. Here she developed her now world-famous teaching method. Possibly Montessori's most revolutionary belief was the importance of the child's environment when learning. She felt that for children to flourish and grow in self-esteem, they needed to work in a child-centered environment. Today, not only Montessori schools, but all schools recognize the part that the environment has to play in the development of the child.

Montessori always claimed that she did not devise a teaching method but that her ideas merely grew out of close observation of children. Montessori principles are based on the needs of the child, including the need to be independent, to find joy in learning, to enjoy order, to be respected and listened to, and to discover both fact and fiction. Today, these needs remain unchanged and are as relevant now as when they were first observed in 1909.

HOW TO USE THIS BOOK

This book is based on key Montessori principles of learning through experience, but rest assured, there is no need to create a Montessori classroom in your own home. The activities require little preparation and use readily available materials. You may be worried that you have no specialist knowledge of teaching; do not worry!

The points set out on the opposite page will guide you through the essential steps when presenting an activity to your child.

A NOTE ON HOW TO HANDLE SCISSORS WITH CHILDREN

Before learning to cut, children need to learn how to handle scissors safely. Teach your child that when carrying scissors, the scissors need to be held with the whole hand wrapped around the closed blades. Show her how to pass the scissors with the handle facing the person receiving them.

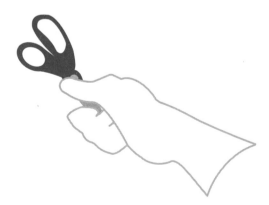

- To avoid repetition, the use of "she" and "he" is alternated in the activities. All the activities are suitable for boys and girls.

- Check your environment. Make sure that you and your child can do the activity in comfort and safety.

- Make sure that your child can see the activity clearly. Sit your child to the left of you (or to your right if she is left-handed).

- Aim to work with your right hand (or your left hand, if your child is left-handed) for consistency.

- Many of the activities are set on a tray. This defines the work space for your child. Choose a tray that is not patterned, to avoid distraction.

- Prepare the activity in advance. There is no point suggesting an activity to a child only to discover that you don't have the materials.

- Be orderly when presenting the activity. Set out your materials in an organized way and this will instill in your child a sense of order.

- Make your child responsible for carrying the materials to the work space and then returning them when the activity is completed. This creates a "cycle of work," and encourages your child to focus on the project.

- Be clear in your own mind of the aim of the activity, so always read through the exercise first.

- Do not interrupt when your child is working. Learn to sit back and observe.

- Try not to be negative. If your child is unable to do the activity correctly, then make a mental note to reintroduce it again at a later stage.

- If your child is absorbed by the activity and wishes to repeat it, let her do so, as many times as she wishes. A child learns through repetition.

- Create a work area for your child, if space permits. When an activity is over, leave the activity in a safe area, so your child can return to it if she wishes.

- If your child abuses any of the materials in the activity, then the activity needs to be removed immediately. By doing this, she will understand that her behavior was unacceptable. The activity can be reintroduced at a later date.

- Remember that at all times you are the role model and your child will model her behavior on your own.

FREQUENTLY ASKED QUESTIONS

How old should my child be before she is presented with an activity?

I have not set ages deliberately, as this can cause panic in parents if their child does not want to do a particular activity. Each child is an individual with different strengths and weaknesses and it is very rare to find a child who is confident in all areas of study. As a guideline, in a Montessori preschool, children are generally introduced to the activities at the beginning of the chapters first, as these make a good foundation for the rest of the activities.

For children aged between four and five, I suggest that you introduce a selection of activities from all the chapters. The exception to this is if your child has a particular interest in a subject, for example, math, in which case you can present more of the numeracy activities.

Do I need to follow the order of the activities?

Aim to take each chapter in the order given, as it follows a natural progression. There is some flexibility; you can try an activity, and then return to it at a later stage, if necessary. If your child already knows the alphabet, or the numerals up to 10, you might be able to introduce a later activity. However, it does not hurt to review knowledge, and this can increase a child's confidence.

If an activity is graded, when can my child progress to the next level of the activity?

In the boxes called "Also try," you will find progression activities that are ordered from easiest to hardest. Once your child has mastered one activity, and she feels confident to work independently, then present the next level of the activity.

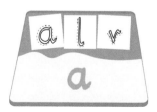

What if my child is confused with the activity?

If your child demonstrates that she is confused with the activity, it is most likely that she is not ready for it. This is particularly the case for language and math activities. Consider also if your own modeling of the demonstration was done slowly and clearly enough and that you fully understood the purpose of the activity.

When is the best time in the day to present the activities?

Children, like adults, are more receptive during certain times of the day. The majority of children are at their most receptive in the morning, so any language and numeracy activities should be done at this time. The other activities can be done at any time, but I would advise against doing them past mid-afternoon.

What if my child does not seem to respond to this activity?

If your child seems to be showing no interest in the activity, do not worry or get cross with your child. Simply put the activity away. Go through the presentation points alone. Ask yourself, did I present the activity in an appealing way? Was it the right time of the day? Did I understand my aim and did my child understand what was required? If it was a language or numeracy activity, consider whether your child was ready for that activity.

How do I use the worksheets?

When using the worksheets at the back of the book, photocopy them onto 11 x 17 in. size paper, enlarging them to fit the full paper size. This way there will be plenty of space for your child to use each worksheet and they can be reused many times over.

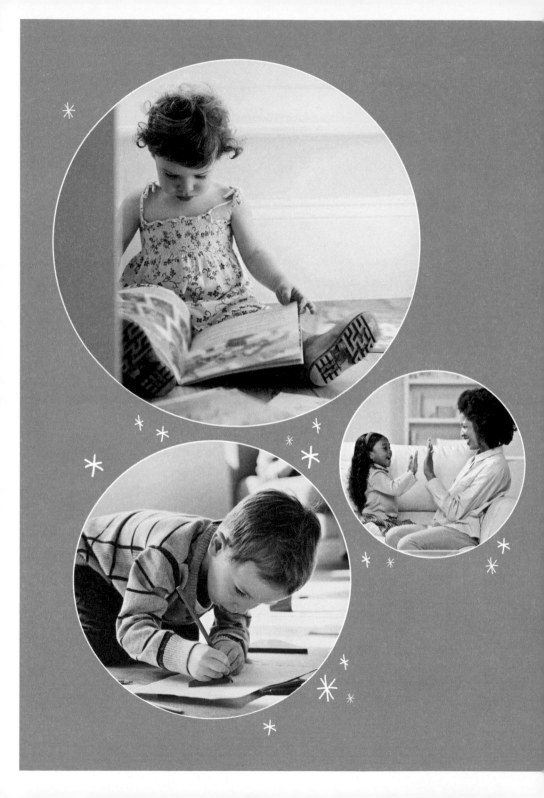

WORD PLAY

Children approach language in a different way to adults. If your child is enjoying an activity, he will "absorb" the words being introduced: it will not seem like hard work. There is no one set formula for developing your child's interest in language. It may develop through an interest in stories, poems, or songs, or in finding out about a favorite topic. The activities in this chapter will help to instill in your child a love of words, language, and books, and when you achieve this, reading will follow naturally.

LEARNING THE NAMES OF COLORS

Children are endlessly fascinated by colors; they play a substantial part in children's developing understanding of the world around them. It makes sense to teach them the names of the colors as soon as possible. This activity is a wonderful way of introducing primary and secondary colors and demonstrates in a very hands-on, concrete way how primary colors are mixed to create secondary colors.

You will need

- Yellow poster paint
- Red poster paint
- Blue poster paint
- 3 resealable plastic bags
- Tray

Activity

1 Put the paint bottles and resealable bags onto a tray.

2 Invite your child to carry the tray to the work area.

3 Explain to your child that he is going to try some paint mixing and that by mixing yellow and blue he is going to make a new color.

4 Ask him to open up a bag while you squeeze in some yellow paint.

5   Trade roles and you hold the bag while your child squeezes in some blue paint.

6   Seal the bag securely and allow your child to mix the paint by rubbing his hands over the bag until the yellow and blue paint mix together to make green.

7   Repeat these steps to make the other secondary colors in the other bags. Mix blue and red to make purple and yellow and red to make orange.

Also try

Go on a color hunt. Write the names of the primary colors separately on large strips of paper. Help your child to read the name of the color (start with red). He then needs to find something in the room that is red and place the color name on it. Once the primary colors have been mastered, move on to the secondary colors.

Introduce the colors of the rainbow.

The ratio of paint should be 2:1 yellow to blue.

If you do not have any poster paint you could use powder paint with cornstarch and water.

THE CLAPPING GAME

This fun game requires no resources, just a pair of hands.
It can be played with one child or as many children as you wish.
While your child is having fun, subconsciously he is developing
an awareness of the rhythms and patterns of speech.

Activity

1 Sit facing your child, or if there is more than one child, in a circle.

2 Start by saying his name out loud and as you do, clap out the name according to the number of syllables. If there is more than one child, go through their names as well.

3 Clap out the names of family and friends.

Instead of hands, you could use things from around the house, such as wooden spoons with pots and pans.

Also try

Try words from other topics familiar to your child. For example you could clap out his favorite animals or things he likes to eat.

LEARNING SIZE AND SHAPE

This simple activity introduces ordering and estimating size and shape as the blocks are built into a tower. In addition, when your child carries the blocks, he will understand that the biggest block is also the heaviest. This activity also introduces the concepts and vocabulary of the words "biggest," "smallest," "bigger," and "smaller."

Show your child that blocks should be carried one at a time. When carrying the bigger blocks, use two hands with one at the bottom and the other spread out over the top.

You will need

- 10 graduated building blocks (ideally, two or three of the blocks should be big enough to require your child to carry them with both hands)

Activity

1 Ask your child to help you take the building blocks to the work area.

2 Sit down with your child so that he can see the blocks clearly.

3 Tell your child that you are going to build the blocks into a tower. Select the largest block and put it in front of you in the center, then slowly complete the rest of the tower.

4 Tell your child that you are going to dismantle the tower so that he can build it. Take down the blocks one at a time and place them to the right of your child. Invite your child to build the tower.

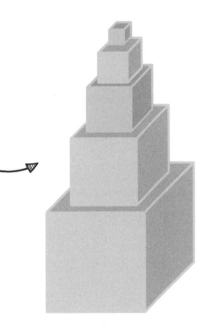

Also try

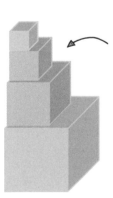

The tower is built again but this time the blocks are placed up one corner rather than centrally.

The blocks are used to build a horizontal stair going left to right, smallest to largest.

STORY GLOVES

Using role play as a means to tell stories is probably one of the most effective ways for children to develop an understanding of how stories are constructed. In this activity a pair of old gloves are transformed into a storytelling tool that can be used for any of their favorite stories.

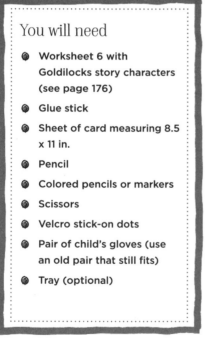

You will need

- **Worksheet 6 with Goldilocks story characters (see page 176)**
- **Glue stick**
- **Sheet of card measuring 8.5 x 11 in.**
- **Pencil**
- **Colored pencils or markers**
- **Scissors**
- **Velcro stick-on dots**
- **Pair of child's gloves (use an old pair that still fits)**
- **Tray (optional)**

Activity

1 Photocopy the worksheet and stick onto the piece of card.

2 Place the card on the table with all the other items on the tray (if using) next to it.

3 Invite your child to come and make some story gloves.

4 Ask her to color in the story characters.

5 Carefully cut out the characters.

6 Stick the Velcro dots onto the gloves and the back of the characters. Your story gloves are now ready to use.

Also try

Make up your own characters from your child's favorite story.

The story gloves can be used for many other stories, here are just a few suggestions: *The Three Billy Goats Gruff; The Three Little Pigs; Little Red Riding Hood.*

Show your child how to do a "rough cut" (roughly cut around each character). Some help may then be needed to trim the edges.

I WENT TO THE STORE AND BOUGHT . . .

You may have played the game as a child where you have to remember a cumulative list of items bought on a supposed shopping trip. This is a simpler version for younger children. It's best played with two or more children.

You will need

- Selection of child-friendly objects (each child should have 1 object to put in the basket)
- Medium-to-large basket
- Towel or cloth large enough to cover the basket

Activity

1 Ask your child to carry the basket, while you carry the other objects to the table.

2 Ask the children to sit in a circle.

3 Tell them that they are going to play a game called I Went to the Store and Bought . . .

4 Put the objects in the center of the circle.

5 Give the basket to the youngest child.

6 Let her choose an object from the selection.

7 When she has chosen, ask her to say, "I went to the store and bought . . ." followed by the name of the object she has selected. Then she puts the object in the basket.

8 The basket is passed around to the next child, who selects another object to put in the basket.

9 When all the objects have been put in, cover the basket with the towel.

Also try

As the children gain more confidence in remembering, you can increase the number of objects each child selects to put in the basket.

10 Ask each child in turn if they can remember what object they bought.

11 When all the children have been asked, uncover the basket so the children can see if they were correct.

If a child is having difficulty remembering, give her some hints, but stress to the other children not to give the answer away.

ALPHABET HUNT

This is another version of hide-and-seek, only it is done with objects. Each object should have the same initial letter sound, so that your child becomes more familiar with the alphabet and the way the letters sound.

A B C D E F G
H I J K L M N
O P Q R S T U
V W X Y Z

You will need

- 4 medium-to-small objects, each with the same initial letter sound, for example, carrot, comb, clip, cup

If you are playing this with more than one child, ensure that there is one object for each child. Ask each child which object they would like to look for. Once they have found their object they could help another child if needed.

Activity

1 Check with your child that he is clear as to what the objects are.

2 Tell him that you are going to hide the objects.

3 Ask him to cover his eyes while you hide the objects.

4 Tell him when you are ready and then ask him to find the objects.

5 If he is having difficulty finding one of the objects, you might need to give him a clue.

6 The game is over when all the objects have been found.

7 Recap the objects and the letter that they start with.

Also try

Once your child is confident finding the objects, you could increase the number of objects to be found.

When this game has been mastered, and as your child becomes more familiar with letters, instead of finding objects that all begin with the same letter, try going through the whole alphabet. Ask your child to find an object that begins with the letter "a," then the letter "b," and so on. Don't go through the whole alphabet at once; try four letters one day, and perhaps the next four letters the following day.

MAKING UP STORIES WITH PROPS

Any prop acts as a great starting point for a story of your child's own making. I have included here some suggestions that I have found work particularly well.

You will need

- Selection of props such as a pair of adult shoes, a variety of hats, or a wrapped-up package with a sign saying "please open me"

Activity

1 Tell your child she is going to make up a story.

2 Show her the prop that you have chosen for her.

3 For the adult shoes, you might like to suggest that they belong to a giant. Ask your child to describe the giant, where he or she lives, and what adventure does he/she go on.

4 For the selection of hats, you might explain to your child that she is going to pretend that the hats belong to some other people. Ask her to describe them and why they wear the hats.

Once upon a time...

Children will need continuous promptings to help them develop the story. Ask questions such as: What happened next? Did they get back safely? Was she scared when she saw the lion?

You will need to act as a guide to bring the story to an end.

5   Children can't resist the appeal of unwrapping a package, so this makes a great starting point for a story. Whatever you put in the package is going to determine the type of story you create. You might put a ring in the package, for example, and explain that the ring has special powers and then ask your child to tell you what they might be and who owns the ring.

SET STORIES WITH PROPS

In this game you are using the props to tell a story with which the child or children are already familiar. They have to guess from the props set out before them which story it is, tell that story, and then act it out. Think of a favorite story and what props you could use to represent the story that your child will instantly recognize and associate with it.

You will need

Props appropriate to the story—for example, for *Goldilocks and the Three Bears*:

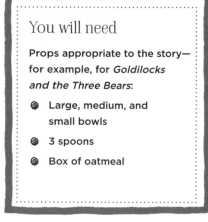

- ● **Large, medium, and small bowls**
- ● **3 spoons**
- ● **Box of oatmeal**

Activity

1   Lay out all of the props you have chosen in front of your child.

2   Ask him what story he knows that includes three bowls of porridge. You might need to point out the different sizes of the bowls to help him.

3   You could then ask why the story is called "Goldilocks and the Three Bears." What does this little girl do?

4   Keep asking questions until your child has told all the main events in the story.

5   Get your child to use the props to mime out the events of the story.

Also try

You can play this activity with any number of children's stories. For example, for *Little Red Riding Hood* you would need props such as a red cape with a hood, or just a red hooded sweater would work well, and a basket of goodies for her to take to Grandma. Ask your child what story includes a red cape. You could then ask why the story is called *Little Red Riding Hood*, what does this little girl do? Again, keep asking questions until he has told all the main events in the story.

STORYBOARD

Here you use pictures cut out from magazines to create a storyboard from which your child can make up his own story. Try to include a number of characters and an interactive setting.

You will need

- Selection of old magazines
- Child's scissors
- Adult scissors
- Black marker
- Sheet of card or paper measuring 11 x 17 in.
- Glue stick

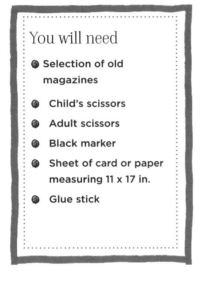

Activity

1 Ask your child to cut out pictures that appeal to him from the magazines. To help him, tear out the page first and circle with the black marker the picture he wishes to cut out.

2 Let him collect about 10 pictures.

3 Ask him to spread out the pictures next to the card.

4 Among the pictures, find one of a person or an animal. If it is a picture of a person, prompt his imagination by asking him what name the person might have. If it is a picture of an animal, ask if the animal is a boy or a girl.

5 Ask him to stick the picture on the top left-hand side of the card, and if you want to, write the name of the person or animal underneath. Tell him that you are going to make up a story about this person or animal.

6 Ask him to look at the other pictures and to tell you what happens next. You may need to make some suggestions to get him started. Does he go on vacation? Does she go shopping?

7 Continue until all the pictures have been used and stuck down in a row across the card. If you don't have enough space, make a second row.

8 Recap the story, picture by picture.

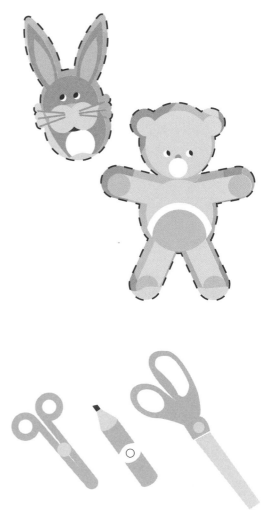

STORY MAPS

Story maps are a great tool to enable children to tell a story and gain a sense of its sequence. This includes understanding that stories have a beginning, a middle, and an end. I have chosen *Goldilocks and the Three Bears*, as it has an excellent use of vocabulary in describing textures, temperatures, and sizes, although feel free to choose whichever story your child particularly likes.

You will need

- **Sheet of paper measuring 11 x 17 in.**
- **Pencil**
- **Colored pencils, crayons, or markers**
- **Eraser**
- **Book of your child's favorite fairy tale (such as *Goldilocks and the Three Bears*)**

Activity

1   Place the paper on the table, either portrait or landscape, with the drawing materials next to it.

2   Invite your child to bring a book of one of her favorite fairy tales to the table and explain to her that she is going to make a story map.

3 Ask her to mark where she thinks the main character's house should be and now ask her to mark in where the other characters would live. Suggest to her that maybe there should be a pathway between the two homes.

4 Ask her what she thinks should be on either side of the pathway. Ask her to draw and color in all these features.

5 With the map complete she can now use it as a tool to retell the story, perhaps starting with "Once upon a time."

Also try

Worksheet 6 with the characters of the Goldilocks story can be photocopied and colored and cut out and mounted onto a card (see page 176). At the bottom of each character card put a small ball of adhesive putty and then they can be placed on the map and moved around as the story is told.

LEARNING TO LOVE BOOKS

Part of fostering a love of stories and literature within your child
is also getting them to treat books with care and respect.
Here are my top tips for encouraging such an attitude:

- Remember that you are the role model: If your child sees you treating books with care then he will do the same.

- Show your child some of your favorite books, especially if they are from your childhood, and explain why they are special to you.

- Demonstrate to your child how to handle books and turn the pages.

- Remind your child that hands need to be clean when handling books and that books should not be marked with any type of pencil or pen.

- For older children ensure that their books are easily accessible and show them how to remove and return a book to a shelf.

- For younger children use book boxes (wooden boxes of books, which are often used by libraries); you could have one box for fiction and one for nonfiction.

SELECTING BOOKS

With such a multitude of children's books to choose from, where do you begin? Here are some guidelines to help you make your selection, whether you are selecting from a bookstore or library.

- Allow yourself as much time as possible. Whenever possible, take your child, so that she can experience the pleasure of browsing through books, which is much more fun than looking online.

- If you are choosing a book for your child to look at, choose one suitable for her age level. When selecting a book for storytelling, select one aimed about a year and a half above your child's age.

- Choose a mixture of short and long stories, and as your child gets older, he could have a bedtime book, with a chapter that is read every night.

- Check to see if the book has any images or ideas that may frighten your child; this is especially important if it is a book for bedtime. Also avoid just glancing at the first two pages; you might be caught out by an unexpected ending.

- Choose books that you know your child has an interest in—for example animals or vehicles. Also consider books that deal with childhood issues like feelings, sharing, and friendship.

- Make sure that there is a balance of books between the fantastical and the everyday, with a wide range of human emotions.

- Nonfiction books are great for dealing with "first time situations" like a new baby in the family, going to the doctor, or the first day at school. They can also be used to explore an interest your child may have—for example dinosaurs—or to answer questions about the world around us.

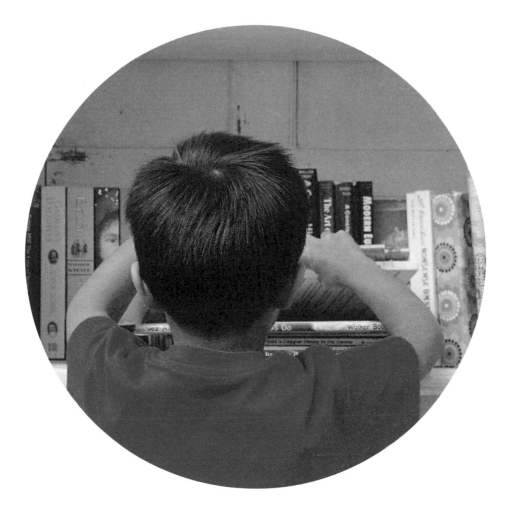

Choose books that contain clear illustrations that illuminate the text, and in the case of fiction, give an idea of the sequence of the story.

Finally, and most importantly, allow your child to have some input into the selection.

READING TO YOUR CHILD

"Are you sitting comfortably? Then I'll begin." That's the way all stories should start, because our enjoyment of a story is increased if we are comfortable and ready to listen. Set aside a time for storytelling, and make sure that when you are reading to your child, he is comfortable and ready. Think about creating a reading corner in his bedroom, with floor cushions and a soft blanket for winter.

How a story is read affects how your child follows and understands it. I suggest that you read the story first. This enables you to check for suitability, but also so you can introduce it, to draw your child in before it starts. For example, "This is my favorite story because . . . " or "This story makes me laugh because . . . " Alternatively, you can tell him about the start of the story, "In this story, a little mouse goes on an adventure; let's see what happens."

With some stories, you may need to reassure your child if there are parts that you think he could find a little scary. For example, in *Little Red Riding Hood,* you could explain that talking wolves only exist in storybooks. For older children you could say, "This story is about a little girl and a wolf, but I think the little girl is going to be smarter; let's find out."

- During the story, ask questions and make comments. If you know that the story is reaching a very exciting part, pause before it to ask your child the possible outcome—for example, "Do you think the little boy is going to be rescued?" If the story is dealing with a childhood issue, such as sharing, you could make a comment on the situation such as, "That wasn't very nice of the little girl not to share her toys."

The End

- By questioning and commenting in this way, your child will want to do the same. Be careful that the questions and comments don't get in the way of the sequence of the story. If you fear that this may be happening, say to your child, "Let's continue the story and we can think about the question when the story is finished." When the story is finished, take time to talk through with your child what he thought about the story and any issues arising from it.

READING WITH YOUR CHILD

Having enjoyed listening to stories being read to him, your child is now ready for his first reading book. There are many books written especially for first-time readers. You will need to select a phonetic-based reading model, where the books are graded carefully, introducing new vocabulary at each level. Choose books that have some of the same nouns that your child may already be able to read. You will find that the books will follow the same structure, and will build through words to phrases and sentences, just as in the activities in this chapter.

● Be very positive and encouraging when presenting a new book to your child. Tell him the title of the book, and discuss from looking at the picture on the cover what the story might be.

● Explain to your child that he is going to start by looking at the pictures. By doing this first, he will get an idea of the story before attempting to read it.

● Tell him that he already knows some of the words in the book. Go through the book and identify words that he is already familiar with. Encourage him to read the words; this will reassure him that he will be able to read the book.

● Go back to the start so that he can read the story. Put your finger under each word that he is reading and ask him to "sound out" the phonic sounds of the individual letters just as he did in the reading activities.

● As he gains confidence, he will begin to recognize the words without the need to sound them out. For new sight words, you will need to read them to your child, but eventually, through repetition, he will begin to recognize them for himself.

- If you want to reinforce key sight words, you could make some flash cards.

- Never be tempted to cover the pictures when your child is reading "to see if he really knows the words." The pictures help to decode the words.

- Spend no longer than 10 minutes on each reading session. Discuss the story with your child and let him ask questions about it.

- When your child completes a book, let him know how pleased you are with his reading.

- Always review and repeat books, and do not be tempted to move on to the next book until your child is confident with reading the present book.

INTRODUCING OUR WORLD

A globe or a map will help your child make his first experience of geography as concrete as possible. Your child will learn to familiarize himself with the globe and world map and come to understand that they both represent our planet, and he will learn that land masses are made up of continents each with their own names.

You will need

- Globe
- World map, preferably one with each continent shown in a separate color

Activity

1   Show your child the globe and invite him to feel around it. Ask him what shape it reminds him of. Hopefully he will say a ball, and you can explain that this shape is called a sphere. He may remember this from earlier activities.

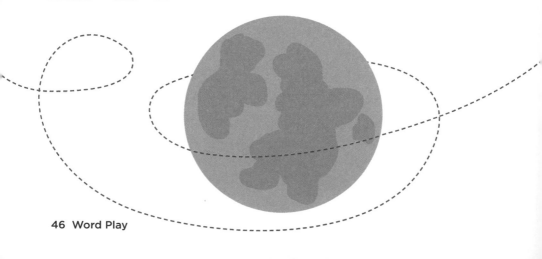

2 Explain that the sphere represents Earth, the planet that we live on. Later on, explain that it is also called a globe. Explain that the blue represents the oceans and the colored shapes represent the land.

3 Show him the country where he lives. Mention your hometown or city, and then explain that it is in a much larger country. Using your finger, trace around the outline of the country and ask him to do the same. As he is doing this, say the name of the country you live in.

4 Now find other destinations that he will be familiar with, like where other family members live or where you have been on vacation. Over the next few days, introduce your child to the rest of the continents.

Also try

Show your child an atlas. Ask him to find your country on the globe, then ask him to find it in the atlas. If he is having difficulty, give him some clues, such as telling him the color of the continent. Repeat, asking him to find other countries he has visited.

If your child loves animals, talk about the different animals found on the continents. Stick pictures onto the map.

As you introduce new countries and continents, review familiar destinations first.

ENJOYING WORD PLAY

Through your storytelling, you have enabled your child to experience the potential excitement of language. Now you can help her to explore the vocal power of words, through their sounds, rhythms, and rhymes.

Nursery rhymes

● The appeal of nursery rhymes is universal; such is the influence of them in our childhood that we remember them as adults. The fact that your child will not understand the original meaning of the rhyme will not deter her enjoyment of it. Part of the appeal of nursery rhymes is the sheer nonsense of the images—Humpty Dumpty on the wall or mice running up a clock, for example.

● Nursery rhymes will introduce your child to words that rhyme, and children find this a very exciting aspect of language. You can expand upon this by looking at the rhyming words in the stories, seeing if you can add to them, or make a nonsense sentence from them. Children also enjoy nursery rhymes with actions, which develop their coordination, as well as reinforce rhymes. To make your child aware of the rhythms in the words, try saying the rhyme with your child to a clapping beat.

Poetry

● The rhymes and play on words in poetry is more intricate than in nursery rhymes. Like stories, poetry can give a child a wider understanding of the world around them, and deal with childhood experiences. Poems and rhymes can also be used as a memory aid for learning topics such as days of the week or months of the year.

Children enjoy learning poetry by heart, and take great pride when they manage to memorize a poem. Start with a poem no more than four lines long, and work up to something longer. Your objective should be to foster enjoyment of language, rather than the mechanics of learning it. Never spend longer than 10 minutes at a time on learning a poem.

As well as memorizing poetry, you could also introduce some tongue twisters, such as "Peter Piper."

Making up stories

By helping your child to make up her own stories, you will be helping her to understand how a story is constructed. Begin by discussing the characters in her story, their names, where they live, and what might happen to them. Tell the story, but stop often to ask your child, "What happens next?" When the story is finished, comment on the ideas that she has used in the story.

THE PHONIC ALPHABET

In Montessori, the phonic sounds of the alphabet are always taught before the names of the letters in the alphabet. As well as teaching the phonic sound of a letter, we also teach how to trace the letter, in the same direction as you would write it. This activity uses salt trays made from baking sheets, because children respond to the tactile feel of the salt, helping them to memorize the tracing direction for that letter. Montessori schools use sandpaper letters; if you are feeling very industrious, you could make your own set of sandpaper letters, using the letters on Worksheet 2 as a guide. Trace around, cut out, and stick them onto thick cardboard.

You will need

- 2 small baking sheets, about 9 x 13 in. (20 x 30 cm)
- Salt to half-fill the sheets
- Worksheet 1, alphabet letters with phonic sounds

Activity

1 Make sure that your child has clean, dry hands. Ask your child to carry one of the trays to the table, while you carry the other. Put one of the trays in front of her and the other on your right.

2 Trace the letter "a," using the full width of the tray to form the letter, and using your index finger. Say its phonic sound (use the worksheet for reference). Pass the tray to your child to trace over the letter, and as she is doing this, say, "This is 'a.'"

3 Trade trays and repeat the same steps for "t." Repeat the same steps again for both letters, to reinforce the work.

Also try

Continue introducing the rest of the phonic alphabet, but always review the two letters from the previous time. Keep a record of the letters you have covered.

4   Put both trays in front of your child and ask her, "Can you show me the 'a' and can you show me the 't'?"

5   Then trade trays, but this time say, "Can you trace the 'a' and can you trace the 't'?" Then ask, "Which one is the 'a' and which is the 't'? Can you trace it?"

6   Point to the "a" tray and ask, "What is this?" After your child has named it, ask her to say the sound again and to trace it. Point to the "t" tray and follow the same steps.

7   Repeat steps 2 to 6, but start with the "t."

Try to encourage your child to say the phonic sound while tracing the letter.

PHONIC SOUND GAMES

Phonic sounds are the building blocks of words and your child learning to identify them is the first step toward learning how to make words. This game helps to reinforce the phonic sounds by using concrete objects, which help your child to feel confident identifying the initial sounds of the object names. I cannot emphasize enough the need to go slowly so that your child correctly hears the sound.

You will need

- 3 to 4 small objects starting with the same phonic sound
- 3 to 4 objects starting with other phonic sounds
- Tray, preferably plain

Activity

1. Place all the objects on the tray.

2. Invite your child to come and sit next to you.

3. Explain to him that he needs to pick out those objects beginning with the phonic sound you have chosen.

4. Say the sound really carefully and ask him to repeat it before he starts finding the objects.

5. As he finds each object, ask him to remove it from the tray and place it to the side.

6. Ask him to repeat the names of each of the objects.

For younger children, check that they know the names of all the objects before starting the game. You could give a demonstration with one or two of the objects.

Also try

Once your child is confident with this game he can progress onto listening for end and middle sounds in the names of objects.

IDENTIFYING LETTERS

These next two activities focus on the written symbols for different letters. In this first activity, you will use a salt tray to write a letter, which then has to be matched to paper letters. As your child becomes more confident identifying letters, you will introduce more letters to choose from.

You will need

- Worksheet 2
- Basket or container
- Baking sheet 9 x 13 in. (20 x 30 cm)
- Salt to half-fill the sheet

Activity

1   Ask your child to carry the basket to the table, while you carry the salt tray. Put the salt tray in front of her and the basket in front of you.

2   Select three letters from the basket, making sure that they contrast in form to each other.

Photocopy the worksheet and cut out the letters following the dotted lines. Put the individual letters into the basket or container and half-fill the baking sheet with salt.

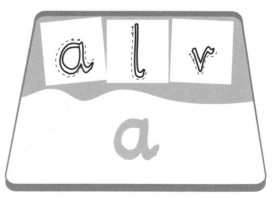

3 Put the letters in a row above the salt. Trace one of the letters in the salt. Ask your child to go over your tracing and then to select the paper letter that matches it.

4 Ask your child to erase the letter from the salt while you select another three letters. Repeat the same steps until you have gone through about eight letters.

MATCHING PAPER LETTERS

In the previous activity, only one pair of letters was matched up; this is now increased to three pairs, then six, and finally eight. You will need two sets of paper letters.

You will need

- Worksheet 2
- Scissors
- 2 small baskets or containers

Activity

1   Ask your child to take one of the baskets to the table, while you take the other. Ask your child to put one of the baskets in front of him and the other basket in front of you.

Photocopy another set of letters. Put each set in a basket or container.

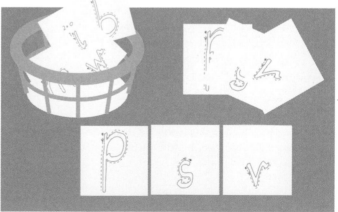

2 Ask your child to take three letters out of his basket and put them in a row at the front of the basket. Find the same three letters from your basket and put them in a pile in front of your child.

3 Ask your child to match up the letters, until all three letters have been paired. Put the paired letters in one pile to the right of you. When the activity is finished, you will need to separate the letters back into the two alphabets.

Also try

Arrange one set of paper letters in rows, in alphabetical order on a large tray. Put the other set in a basket. Ask your child to take a letter out of the basket and pair it up with the one on the tray. You may need to give some clues such as, "I think you will need to have a look in the top row."

WORD BUILDING

This activity is an essential step toward the final goal of reading. Through listening to the phonic sounds of letters, your child will build words aurally and visually.

You will need

- Worksheet 2
- Worksheet 4
- Scissors
- 2 envelopes
- Large tray
- Adhesive putty

Photocopy Worksheet 2 onto paper measuring 11 x 17 in. five times (if you have some alphabet letters from the previous activities they can be reused). Stick one sheet onto the tray using adhesive putty and cut the rest of them up into individual letters. Put the letters in piles onto the tray to match the alphabet sheet.

Photocopy Worksheet 4 onto paper measuring 11 x 17 in. Cut out the words and pictures and put them into phonic sound groups. Put each group in a separate envelope. Choose one envelope at a time for the activity. Use the pictures first; the words are used later.

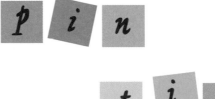

Activity

1   Ask your child to carry one envelope to the floor while you carry the tray. Work on a carpeted area but make sure it is not patterned as this can be distracting. Put the tray in front of your child. Place the envelope in front of you.

2   Take three pictures from the envelope and put them in front of your child. Ask her to choose one of the pictures—for example, the pin. Say to your child, "We are going to build the word 'pin' using the letters." Ask her to put the picture on her left, just below the tray.

3   Now say, "What is the first sound you can hear when I say the word 'pin?'" Get her to say the word with you several times, with each phonic sound spoken slowly and clearly. Help her to put an emphasis on the first sound only.

4   When she says "p," ask her to find the letter "p" from the alphabet tray and put the letter next to the picture.

continues on next page ➞

This is an activity that demands careful listening to the individual sounds of the word, so take time to say the phonic sounds of the words slowly and clearly.

5 Now say to your child, "We have the 'p' but now we need to listen for the next sound." Repeat the same steps as before, to find the "i," placing it next to the "p."

6 Your child may go straight to the end sound of "n" (children find it much easier to hear the beginning and end sounds in words). If this happens, follow the same steps, but when she puts the letter "n" next to "p," ask her to leave a space. Tell her that she needs to listen to find another letter to go between the "p" and "n."

7 Ask your child, "Can you listen for the last sound in 'pin?'" Follow the same steps until the "n" letter is found and put it next to the "p" and the "i" to make "pin."

Also try

Repeat with a second and third word from the same vowel group. Use words with three letters—for example "tin" and "pip."

When your child has completed three words, ask her if she would like to build a fourth word. Gradually build this to six words, but only increase the number at her pace.

When your child has completed one vowel group, go onto another one. Because it will be a new vowel sound, work with her for the first one or two words and then let her complete the whole six.

Introduce four-letter phonic words. You could prepare the word and picture worksheet for this, following the pattern of Worksheet 4.

READING USING WORD AND PICTURE CARDS

The same picture cards that were used in the previous activity are used again, but this time they help to decode the written word. Your child will need to have completed the previous activity before attempting to read the cards.

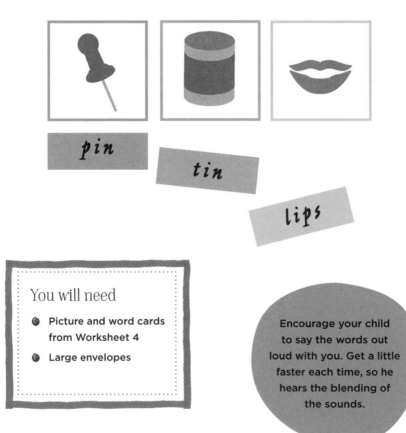

You will need

- Picture and word cards from Worksheet 4
- Large envelopes

Encourage your child to say the words out loud with you. Get a little faster each time, so he hears the blending of the sounds.

Activity

1   Choose one group of the picture and word cards (for example, all using the same vowel in them), and ask your child to carry the envelope to the table.

2   Take out three pictures and ask your child to put them in a row in front of him in the middle of the table. While he is doing that, find the matching word cards and put them together in a pile in front of your child.

3   Ask your child to read the first word. He will need to go slowly through the individual sounds. Ask him what is the first sound of the word. Tell him to look for a picture that begins with that sound and, if necessary, take him through each of the pictures, asking him to tell you its first sound. When he has read the word, ask him to put it under the picture.

Also try

When your child is confident matching the words with the pictures, increase the number of pictures to six. You can use the previous three cards again, as it is good to have a mixture of the familiar with the new.

Let your child work through the other vowel groups.

4   Follow the same steps until all the word cards are read and there is a row of pictures with their words underneath. If your child is stuck on one of the words, say to him, "We will come back to this word." Put the word to the bottom of the pile so it can be attempted again at the end.

CONSTRUCTING PHRASES

Your child will enjoy this activity because the phrase that she constructs can be as nonsensical as she wishes. Through the word-building and reading activities, your child will have learned to construct and read three- and four-letter phonic words. The next activity shows how to use these words in the context of a phrase and, overleaf, in a sentence. It also introduces sight words, words that cannot be "sounded out" but must be learned by sight, such as "the."

You will need

- Worksheet 3
- Set of three-letter picture and word cards from Worksheet 4
- Scissors
- 3 envelopes
- Colored pencils

Photocopy Worksheet 3 twice, and shade each column a different color: blue for the articles and yellow for the verbs. Shade lightly, so as not to obscure the word. Cut out the individual words and put them in separate envelopes to the pictures.

Activity

1   Put the envelopes on the tray. Ask your child to carry the tray to the table and to sit on your left. With the tray in front of your child in the middle, ask her to choose three picture cards from the picture envelope and put them in a row in front of her.

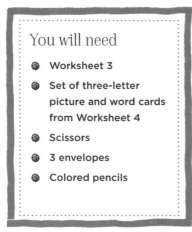

Keep the noun picture and word cards in a separate envelope from the other parts of speech.

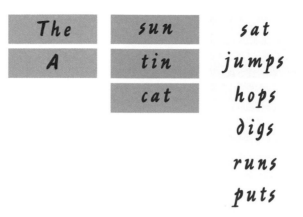

The	sun	sat
A	tin	jumps
	cat	hops
		digs
		runs
		puts

2 From the word envelope, take out the verbs and the two "the" and "a" cards, and arrange them on the tray in vertical columns. Add the three noun cards that match the pictures your child has chosen. Put the envelope to your right.

3 Ask your child to choose one of the pictures and put it just below the tray in the middle. Ask him to identify the picture, and to find the matching word on the tray. (You will need to point out to him where the column of nouns is.) Ask her to place it under the picture.

4 Ask your child to choose what the word is doing. For example, if she chose "cat," ask what the cat could be doing. Show him the column of verbs to read through with your guidance. Ask her to select one and put it after the noun. Follow the same steps for the other two pictures.

Also try

When your child can construct three phrases, use three other picture cards in that group. Continue with the rest of the vowel groups, and finally move on to the four-letter words, always working in groups of three.

5 Return to the first picture, and explain that all naming words need to have "the" or "a" before them. Go on to give an example, such as, "The frog hops." Ask your child to choose "the" or "a" for her sentence. (At this stage, do not worry about teaching the correct context for using "the" or "a.") Follow the same steps to add "the" or "a" to the other two phrases.

MAKING A SENTENCE

When your child is confident constructing a phrase, he can try building the phrase into a sentence. In this activity, he will add an adjective, preposition, second article, and second noun. Part of the enjoyment of this activity is that your child can construct sentences as nonsensical as he wishes; there is no need for the sentence to make sense. This is a difficult activity, so when your child has completed it, let him know what a good job he has done.

You will need

- Paper
- Black marker
- Word cards from Worksheets 3 and 4

Wait until your child is fully confident in one stage of this activity before introducing a new concept.

Activity

1 Follow the same steps as on the previous activity, but this time add adjectives to the phrases. Tell your child that they are "describing" words. Leave a space between "the" or "a" and the noun. Say, "We are going to add a new word that describes our . . . " (for example, "cat").

2 Follow the same steps, but this time add prepositions to the phrases. After your child has added the adjectives, say, "We are going to add a new word that tells you where the cat sat."

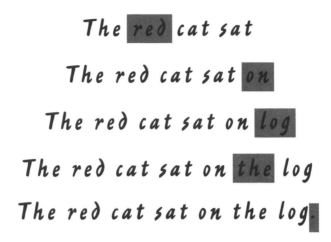

The red *cat sat*

The red cat sat on

The red cat sat on log

The red cat sat on the *log*

The red cat sat on the log.

3 Follow the same steps, but now add a second noun. After your child has added the prepositions, say, "We are going to add a new word that tells you what the cat sat on." Leave space between the preposition and the noun.

4 Follow the same steps, but this time, add the second "the" or "a." After your child has added the noun, he might realize why a space has been left before it. If not, point to the first noun and the "the" or "a" before it. Remind your child that he needs a "the" or "a."

5 When your child has constructed the sentence, explain that you have made a sentence and review all the steps he went through. You can even add a paper dot to represent the full stop. Let your child go on to turn the other two phrases into sentences.

Remember that the sentences don't have to make complete sense at this stage; the point is to understand the meaning of "sentence."

MAKING A DIARY

Creating a diary is a very good way for children to understand the idea of sequence. You could save this activity until you are on vacation, or simply record the events of a normal week.

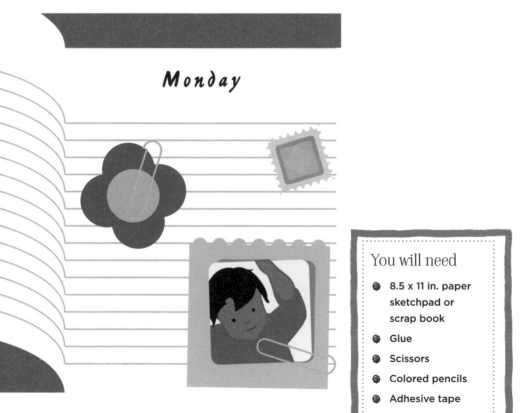

Monday

You will need

- 8.5 x 11 in. paper sketchpad or scrap book
- Glue
- Scissors
- Colored pencils
- Adhesive tape
- Small clear bags

Activity

1 On the first page, write "My Diary." If your child is old enough, she could write it herself. Write the day, and the date at the top of each page to make a full week.

2 Each day, help your child to gather and collect items that she could put in her diary. For example, postcards, shells, leaves, feathers, flowers, wrappers, tickets, and photographs.

3 Encourage your child to put the item in the diary on the day it happens or else she may forget which day she collected it. For items like shells or feathers, put them in small clear bags and stick or staple them in. If there was a day when nothing was collected, your child could draw a picture of what she did that day.

4 Older children should be encouraged to write a sentence or two underneath. When the diary is complete, review it with your child, going through each day to see if she can remember what happened. Give her time to look at the pictures or items before she comments.

MAKING A BOOK

The most obvious way for your child to understand how a story is constructed is to make a book. This activity uses the "story" of the life cycle of the butterfly, as this has a natural progression. Before your child makes his book, he will need to be familiar with the life cycle. One of the best ways is to see the cycle in action. You can obtain caterpillar eggs by mail, complete with the correct food and environment so that your child can witness the events at close hand. If this is not possible, look at a book together so that your child can see the different stages of the cycle.

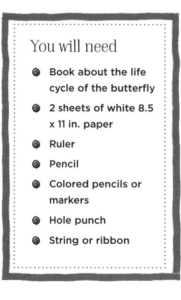

You will need

- Book about the life cycle of the butterfly
- 2 sheets of white 8.5 x 11 in. paper
- Ruler
- Pencil
- Colored pencils or markers
- Hole punch
- String or ribbon

Using your ruler and pencil, divide the paper into six equal squares.

Activity

1   Tell your child that he is going to make his own book about the life cycle of the butterfly. Help him to draw a different stage of the cycle in each square.

2   Ask your child to shade in, and cut out, the pictures and to stick one on each page.

3   If your child is old enough, encourage him to write a sentence or two about each picture.

4   Provide another sheet of paper or card to make a front cover. Hole-punch each sheet of paper, and show your child how to put the whole book together with a piece of string or ribbon. Ask your child to decorate the cover.

An egg on a leaf

A baby caterpillar

A big caterpillar eating leaves

A caterpillar building a cocoon

A butterfly emerging from the cocoon

A butterfly drying its wings

Also try

Eric Carle's *The Very Hungry Caterpillar* is a fictional account of the life cycle of the butterfly. The caterpillar eats its way through an assortment of food, including lollipops and cheese. Your child could change this to foods of his own choosing. Your child might like to add holes to his book, also.

CREATING A FAMILY TREE

Through the experience of creating a family tree, your child will learn about where she fits into her family, and come to understand the terms past, present, and future.

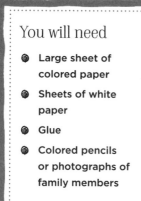

You will need

- Large sheet of colored paper
- Sheets of white paper
- Glue
- Colored pencils or photographs of family members

Activity

1 On the large sheet of colored paper, ask your child to draw a large tree to fill the whole page. Tell your child that she is going to make a family tree.

2 On one white sheet of paper, ask your child to draw a picture of each family member, or to find photographs.

3 Help your child to stick the pictures or photographs onto the tree, with the grandparents at the top, parents in the middle, and children at the bottom. You may also like to include aunts, uncles, cousins, and even pets.

4 Ask your child to write "My Family Tree" at the top of the sheet. She could also name all the family members, add their birth dates, and add arrows pointing to their picture.

MAKING A PICTURE POEM

This activity is a change from structured story writing and allows your child to discover just how much fun language can be. In a picture poem, the words form the actual shape of the subject of the poem. Almost any subject works. Here are some examples.

Snail poem

Ask your child to write the words of a poem following the spiral curl of a snail's shell. Encourage him to use "s" words to match the snail, like "slippery" and "slidey."

leaves a trail
slidey snail
slippery?

When your child has decided on the subject of his poem, read him other poems on that subject to give him some ideas. Then help him to write down his ideas and to look at ways to form the words into the shape of the subject.

Sea poem

Ask your child to write the words of the poem to make waves, using "w" words like "wet" and "windy."

Moon poem

Ask your child to write the poem to form the shape of a crescent moon, using words describing its silvery light.

Animal poem

This could be about the movement of an animal, such as a hopping rabbit.

SAY "HELLO" FROM AROUND THE WORLD

It has already been mentioned how Montessori observed that children seem to have a capacity to absorb language, and I can certainly testify to numerous bilingual and trilingual children I have taught who switched between languages with complete ease. For children and adults alike, the best place to start when introducing a child to another language is with a simple "Hello."

You will need

- Favorite toy
- Atlas or globe

It is a good idea to introduce your child to an atlas so she can learn about the countries first.

Also try

If your child has friends in her class who speak other languages, find out what the languages are and how to say "hello" in that language.

If you are actually going on vacation abroad, then introduce other greetings as well as hello. You could also introduce the words for colors and foods and learn songs.

Activity

1   Invite your child to come and play the game of "say hello."

2   Ask her to bring her favorite toy to play the game too and an atlas.

3   Say to your child, "let us pretend we are going on vacation to . . . ," saying the name of the country whose language you are learning.

4   Open the atlas and show her where that country is.

5   Tell your child that she and her favorite toy are going on vacation to that country and she will need to know how to say "hello."

6   Tell your child the word for "hello" in that country's language and ask her to repeat it to her toy.

FIND THE MISSING LETTER

This activity focuses on finding the middle sound of a word, which some children find difficult. Before attempting this activity, your child should be reasonably confident with reading three- and four-letter phonic words and should have started forming their letters.

You will need

- **Sheet of paper measuring 8.5 x 11 in.**
- **Pencil**
- **Ruler**

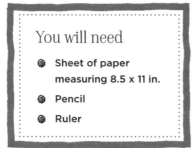

You can find lists of phonic words online; these are known as CVC (consonant, vowel, consonant) words.

For younger children you could start with just five words and then increase the number the next time.

Activity

1 Start by drawing a horizontal line across the page two-thirds down.

2 On the bottom section of the page, write out six to eight three-letter phonic words in two columns (for help, see the note on phonics, below left).

3 On the top part of the page in large letters write out each of the words again, but this time leave a space instead of the middle letter.

4 Draw boxes around each of the letters including the space for the missing letter.

5 Invite your child to come and join you in this activity. Ask him to read through the words at the bottom of the page.

6 Explain that the words at the top of the page are the same but their middle sound is missing.

7 Demonstrate by reading the first word out loud, looking for it at the top and then writing the missing letter with your pencil. Cross off the word at the bottom once it has been found.

8 Hand the pencil to your child and ask him to complete the rest of the words.

Also try

Increase the length of the words from three to four letters.

Leave out end sounds rather than middle sounds.

Choose words that are missing the same letter but in different places in the word.

THANK-YOU NOTES

When I was a teacher, I would suggest to the children at the end of each day that they should count at least five things that had happened for them to say "thank you." The purpose of this was to instill in the children an awareness and a sense of gratitude for all they received. The act of writing a thank-you note in this activity helps to reinforce this awareness. See the tip box for suggestions that will help your child actively enjoy this task.

You will need

- Sheet of notepaper
- Envelope
- Camera
- Pencil
- Ruler
- Sheet of scrap paper
- Selection of colored markers or colored pencils (optional)

Activity

1 Talk to your child about a present he received, for example a birthday present.

2 Take a photo of your child with his present and then print it out.

3 On your scrap paper write out some of the words that your child may need for the letter, such as dear, thank you, present, etc.

4 Draw horizontal lines onto the notepaper, setting it out like a letter

5 Talk to your child about the things he would like to say in his note.

6 At the bottom of the paper leave space to stick down the photo and ask him to write the name of the person on the front of the envelope.

Take your child to a stationery store and let him choose the notepaper; in doing this he will feel much more involved with the activity.

Also try

For older children this is a good opportunity to show them how to write out an address.

As children get older encourage them to start using descriptive words explaining why they like their present.

CONSONANT BLENDS

Once your child is secure in reading and sounding out all the phonic alphabet, it is time to introduce consonant blends. Consonant blends are where two or more phonic sounds come together to make a new sound, such as when "t" and "h" combine to form "th." The English language is full of blends and once your child can learn and understand blends, it will take her level of reading to a new level. We begin with introducing two letter blends at the start of words.

You will need

- Sheet of paper measuring 8.5 x 11 in.
- Pencil
- Ruler
- 2 squares of card in any color about 2 in. (5 cm)

For younger children, start by writing three words and work up to six.

Activity

1   On the paper draw six evenly spaced horizontal lines of about 3-¼ in. (8 cm).

2   Leaving a little space at the front of each line write out on each line: op, oe, ed, e, ell, eep.

3   Place the paper, pencil, and pieces of card in the center of the table. Invite your child to join you and say, "Now that you have learned all the alphabet sounds we are going to learn that sometimes when you put two sounds together they make a new sound."

4   On one of the pieces of card ask your child to write a capital "S" and on the other card ask her to write a lowercase "h." Bring the two cards together and say, "When s and h come together they make 'sh.'" While saying the sound place your finger to your lips to emphasize it.

5   Place the paper in front of her and say, "We are going to write the 'sh' sound in front of each of these group of letters to make words starting with 'sh.'"

6   For each word, ask her to write "sh" before the letter group and then ask her to read the completed word.

Also try

Start with blends at the beginning of words, then at the end of words and then in the middle.

Once she has learned three or more blends, you could change this activity to choose which is the correct consonant blend for the start of the word.

RHYMING WORDS

Rhyming words are an excellent way for children to understand how language is constructed. You will have observed that when your child is saying a nursery rhyme they are able to anticipate the matching rhyming word. In this activity your child will be able to get to grips with the construction of the rhyming word and go on to build the chosen words into a phrase or a sentence.

You will need

- **Sheet of paper measuring 8.5 x 11 in.**
- **Pencil**
- **Ruler**

Activity

1 With the paper placed horizontally, draw a straight horizontal line through the middle of the page.

2 In the top half draw four evenly spaced horizontal lines of about 2 in. (5 cm).

3 On each of the lines, leave a space and then write "at."

Also try

Once she is confident in reading the four words, ask her to think of any other rhyming words that end with "at." From there she could try to construct a phrase or sentence.

Repeat this activity using other vowels.

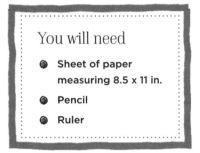

	at
	at
	at
	at
C M R S	

4 On the bottom half of the page with spaces in between write these capital letters: C, M, R, S.

5 Invite your child to the table and ask her to read the letters at the top of the page.

6 Draw her attention to the letters at the bottom. Ask her to choose one and write it before the first "at" and then to read the complete word. Ask her to complete the three remaining words in the same way.

It may be helpful to ask her to draw pictures underneath the words.

OPPOSITES

Our language is infused with opposites, for example, black and white, wide and narrow, soft and hard, up and down. For children opposites are a very good starting point to extend their vocabulary. Once they have grasped the concept of the opposite, then you can introduce more subtle distinctions such as hot, hotter, hottest. For this activity, I use the opposites of big and little, but you can use this activity to apply for most opposites.

You will need

- 8 to 10 objects of big and little sizes
- Tray
- 2 lengths of string, about 3 ft. (1 m) each

For younger children start with fewer objects and then work up to 10.

Activity

1   Invite your child to come and join you in an activity called "opposites."

2   Ask him to put all the objects onto the tray.

3   Ask him to put the tray in the middle in front of him and to make a circle with each piece of string on either side of the tray.

4   Explain that he needs to find little objects to place in the circle on the right and big objects to place in the circle on the left.

5 Demonstrate this with two or three of the objects and then let him complete the activity.

6 Put the objects back on the tray and then let your child do the whole activity by himself.

Also try

Once your child has got the concept of big and little, introduce other words to describe them, such as tiny, small, enormous, huge, etc.

You could ask your child to grade the little objects from little to littlest and then the big objects from big to biggest.

Action songs are a great way to introduce opposites, for example "Incy Wincy Spider" for up and down.

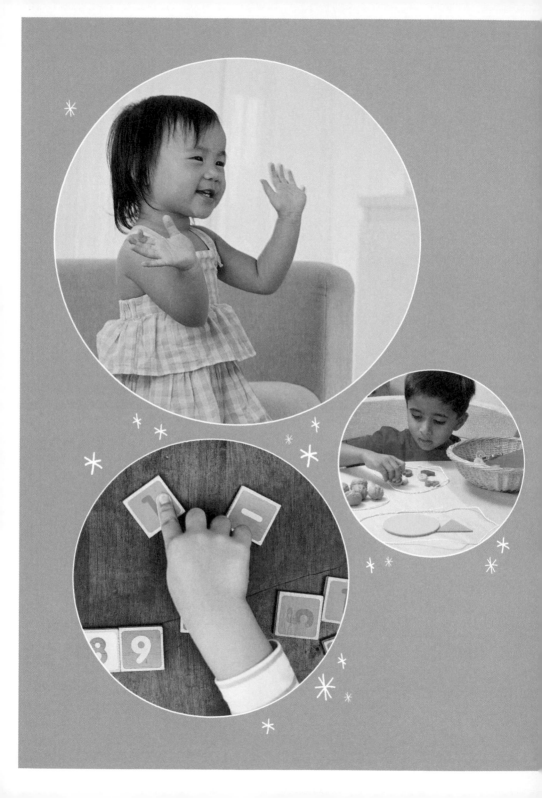

FUN WITH NUMBERS

Montessori observed that mathematics is an abstract concept and for children to be able to understand it, it needed to be made as concrete as possible. The activities in this chapter follow this principle; they start with concrete examples and move toward the abstract. Parents are often surprised that children can find numbers thrilling. Children view math problems like magic spells, and they take great comfort from the fact that 2 + 2 = 4, and that it will always make four. Also included are number games that will engage your child so that she will not even be aware that she is learning math.

PREPOSITIONS

Think about how often you use prepositions (on, under, with, by, etc.) when talking to your children, for example, "you will find your coat on the hook *next to* . . . " They are an essential part of your child's vocabulary and this activity introduces them in a fun way that will allow your child to take the role of the "teacher," which she will really enjoy. Prepositions can be used in a language or math context but are most generally used in math as they describe a spatial distance.

You will need

- 🌀 **Soft toy**
- 🌀 **Chair or table**

Activity

1   Ask your child to find a favorite soft toy.

2   Explain to her that you would like to show her a new game in which she will need to listen very carefully.

3   Ask her to put the toy under the chair or table, then ask her to put the toy on top of the chair or table.

4   Continue in this way, introducing other prepositions such as above, below, near, far, next to, against, etc.

5   When she feels confident with the activity, trade roles so that she gives you the instructions for where to move the toy.

For younger children, before doing this activity introduce the preposition words with a "follow the leader" game where they have to copy your actions; ask if she can put her hands above her head, below her knees, etc.

Also try

Introduce a second toy and ask your child to then compare which toy is closer to the chair or table or farther away from it.

SORTING INTO SETS

This is a simple activity that requires sorting objects into matching sets. When your child has grasped this concept, you can progress to sorting objects by color, shape, and size.

You will need

- **4 sets of small objects (for example, pencils, beads, clothespins, buttons, etc.)**
- **Basket or container to hold objects**
- **4 lengths of string, about 20 in. (50 cm) each**

Activity

1 Ask your child to carry the basket to a carpeted area on the floor or a large table and to sit next to you. Put the basket in front of your child and ask him what objects are in the basket. Explain that the objects are all mixed up and need to be sorted into sets.

2 Take your lengths of string and make circles around the outside of the basket or container. Put one of each object into each circle.

3 Ask your child to sort the rest of the objects into the circle of string.

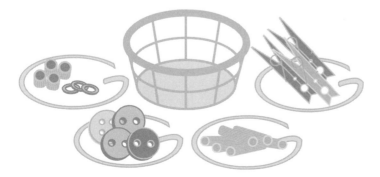

LEARNING 1 TO 10

Number rods are used in Montessori education to teach what the quantity of each number represents. The "Also try" section reinforces this work by sorting with numbers and spotting the "odd quantity out." Please note that the language changes as the activity progresses; this helps your child to understand further the concept of quantity.

You will need

- Number rods (see Worksheet 5)
- 11 x 17 in. paper
- Large sheet of thick cardboard
- Tray

Photocopy and enlarge the worksheet onto 11 x 17 in. paper. Color in the sections blue and red, starting with red for the single section, then blue for the longest section. The first rod will have one section, the second, two (one of each color), the third, three sections, and so on. Cut out the rods and stick them onto the card. Then cut them out, as shown overleaf.

Activity

1   Put the first two number rods onto the tray and ask your child to carry the tray to the table.

2   Take rod 1 and put it in front of your child. Put your index finger on it and say, "This is one." Repeat the same steps with rod 2. Ask your child to repeat the number as you say it. Repeat twice more, using both rods.

Make sure that your child always points at the number and says it out loud.

If your child cannot remember the name of the number, go back to an earlier stage.

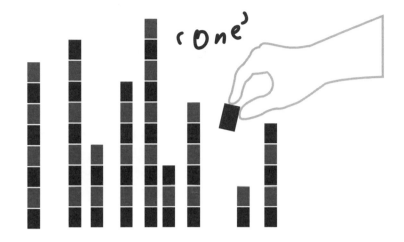

'One'

3 Put both rods in front of your child, and say to her, "Can you point to the one?" Encourage her to put her finger on it. Repeat with two. Switch and rods around, and repeat the same steps but say, "Show me . . . ' Repeat for a third time, but say, "Which is the . . . '

4 Place both rods in front of your child, and put your finger on the 1. Say, "What is this?" She should reply, "One." Now put your finger on the 2 and ask, "What is this?" She should reply, "Two."

5 Encourage your child to count both rods, and to say, "One, two."

6 Switch the rods around and repeat the same steps twice more.

Also try

Teach the quantities up to 10 using the number rods. First introduce three, four, and five, then six, seven, and eight, and finally nine and 10. Each time, review the numbers from the previous session.

As your child begins to recognize number quantities, introduce counting groups of objects (you could use the sets from the previous activity). Ask, "Which set has the largest number of objects?," "Which set has the smallest number of objects?," and "Which set has an equal number of objects to another?"

INTRODUCING NUMBERS BEYOND 10

In Montessori, numbers beyond 10 are introduced using a 10-bead gold-colored bar for tens and the units by beads color coded for each number. This activity replicates this idea, but here the beads for the tens bar are threaded onto a pipe cleaner and the unit beads are loose. As with previous number activities, the quantities are introduced first and then the numerals.

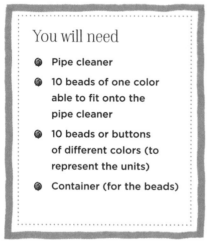

You will need

- Pipe cleaner
- 10 beads of one color able to fit onto the pipe cleaner
- 10 beads or buttons of different colors (to represent the units)
- Container (for the beads)

Activity

1 Put the pipe cleaner in the middle of the table and the beads in the container on the left-hand side.

2 Invite your child to come and join you and explain that you are going to be exploring numbers bigger than 10.

3 Ask him to thread the 10 beads of one color onto the pipe cleaner and place in the center of the table. Explain that these beads represent a 10.

4 Now ask him to count out loud the numbers from 10 to 15 as a reminder of the sequence.

5 Now ask him what number comes after 10. Hopefully he will respond with 11.

6 Ask him to put one bead on the table to the right of the 10 bar and explain that 10 plus one more makes 11. Repeat steps 5 and 6 for the numbers 12 to 15, putting out an extra bead each time. Stop after 15 and then do the numbers 16 to 20 in another session.

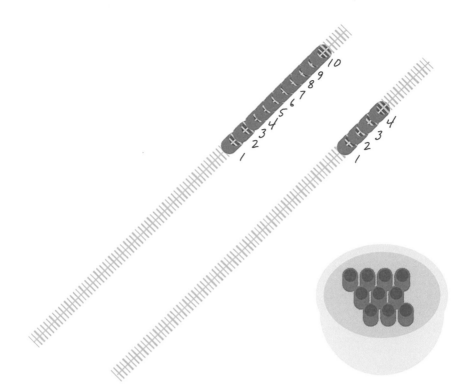

For younger children or for those children less confident, introduce three new numbers in each session and each time review the previous numbers before introducing the next ones.

Also try

Once your child is confident with the numbers 11 to 20 using quantities, introduce him to the numerals using number cards (see page 100). Use the same steps with a 10 card on the left and the unit card on the right.

Do the same sequencing activities as for numbers 1 to 10 (see page 100).

OBJECTS ON A LINE

This activity reinforces the concept of quantities up to 10. You need to collect lots of small objects for this activity, so I suggest you involve your child as you "count up" objects. Look for favorite objects that your child will enjoy displaying on a line across her room.

You will need

- 10 large clear food bags
- 10 clothespins
- Assortment of objects grouped in quantities of one to 10, such as 1 small teddy bear, 2 toy cars, 3 feathers, 4 shells, etc.
- Length of string to extend across a room
- Tray

Activity

1 Put all the objects, food bags, and clothespins onto a tray, and ask your child to carry the tray to the table. Ask your child to sit where she can see clearly.

2 Tell your child that she is going to make a number line, starting from one and going to 10.

3 Ask her to sort the objects into sets. Ask your child to find the set with only one object and to put it in one of the bags. Show your child how to roll over the top of the bag and seal it using the clothespin. Put the bag at the top of the table.

4   Now ask her what number comes after
    one. (If she can't remember, give her
    any two objects to count, and this
    should jog her memory.)

5   Ask her to find the set with two objects,
    and to put them in the bag and close it
    up. Repeat the same steps for the rest
    of the numbers up to 10.

6   Tell your child that she is going to
    display the bags on a number line. Put
    the bags back on the tray, and ask your
    child to take them to the prepared line.
    Ask her to find the bag with one object
    and pass it to you so that you can hang
    it on the line on the left-hand side.
    Repeat until all the bagged objects are
    on the line in a row from one to 10.

Hang the string at a level
that your child can see the
objects. Make sure that it
does not become
an obstruction.

Use large bags so that
the objects fit.

REINFORCING THE SEQUENCE OF NUMERALS

This game will help to reinforce the numerals and sequence of 0 to 10.
It also acts as a guide to how confident your child is in these areas.
In addition, your child will practice using the words
"before" and "after."

You will need

- **Large sheet of card**
- **Black marker**
- **Scissors**

Activity

1   Write the numerals 0 to 10 on the card, allowing space to cut them into squares.

2   Ask your child to carry the number cards to the table. Put the numbers in front of your child in a row, from left to right, in numerical order.

3   Point to a number and ask your child to tell you what the number is. Then ask her what the number is before and after it.

For younger children, just start with the numerals up to five, and then progress on to 10 at a later stage.

Write the numerals 0 to 10 on the card, allowing space to cut them into squares

0 1 2 3 4 5 6 7 8 9 10

4 Repeat several times, pointing to different numbers until all the numbers have been covered. You can also ask questions such as, "Which is the bigger number, eight or ten?" or "Which is the smaller number, three or four?"

Also try

When your child is confident with the sequence of numbers, repeat the game, but this time turn over the numbers before and after, so your child cannot use them as reference. When she guesses, turn them over to show her whether she is correct.

Put the numbers in a row left to right, in numerical order. Remove three of the numbers and turn them face down. Ask your child to turn over one of the numbers and find where it should go in the sequence. Repeat with the other two numbers. As your child gains more confidence, remove more numbers out of the sequence.

TRACING NUMERALS IN SALT TRAYS

Montessori observed that children under the age of seven have heightened senses and this is particularly the case with their sense of touch. The tracing numerals activity draws on this by getting your child to practice writing his numerals in salt with his fingers. This method also has the advantage of allowing your child to erase their numeral easily and try again.

You will need

- Baking sheet
- Shallow tray
- Salt
- Set of number cards 0 to 10 (see page 100)
- Tray

Activity

1 Put the baking sheet onto the other tray to help capture any salt that falls over the edge. Fill the baking sheet with a thin layer of salt.

2 Place the trays in the center of the table with the number cards to the left.

3 Invite your child to the table and explain that he is going to practice tracing the shape of the numerals in the salt.

4 Invite your child to choose a number from the cards and ask him to place it above the tray.

5 Ask him to trace his chosen numeral in the salt. Let him practice tracing the numeral at least three times.

6 Ask him to put away the number card and choose another to trace. Practice three to five numerals in one session.

For younger children practice two to three numerals in any one session and ensure that you review the activity when starting the next session.

Also try

When your child is ready you can reinforce double figures using the same method.

MORE SEQUENCING GAMES

Children learn by repetition, and I find little and often is the best approach. This is certainly to be recommended for learning number sequencing. Following the Montessori pattern, this activity starts with quantities by using a domino set and when this is mastered, swaps to numerals and then combines the two.

You will need

- Set of double-10 dominoes

For younger children, have a shorter sequence up to six and then work up to 10.

Activity

1 Set out the dominoes from left to right in the correct number sequence from one up to 10.

2 Now remove the multiples of two (two, four, six, eight, 10) and place them in a random order to the left of the sequenced dominoes.

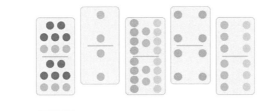

3 Invite your child to complete the sequence with the missing dominoes.

4 Ask her to count the dots starting with the one and the three: She should spot that the two is missing.

5 Ask her to find the two domino from the tiles on the left and put it into the sequence.

6 Repeat step 5 to find the four, six, eight, and 10 until the sequence is complete.

Also try

Repeat this activity, but this time do it with multiples of three and then again with random numbers.

Go beyond 10 if your child feels confident with her numbers.

MORE THAN, LESS THAN

Most children understand the concept of "more than," particularly in reference to food. In math, introducing children to the concept of more than and less than is excellent preparation for the trickier math operations of addition and subtraction. This activity starts by using only quantities and then extends to using numerals as well.

You will need

- **10 to 20 small objects, such as buttons, counters, clothespins, etc.**
- **Tray or container**

Choose numbers between one and 10 and for younger children between one and six.

Do not be tempted to introduce more than and less than together.

Activity

1   Put all your small objects on a tray or in a container and ask your child to take them to the table.

2   Explain to him that you both are going to think about the idea of *more than*.

3   Ask your child to count out a number of objects (let him choose a number below five).

4   Ask him to choose a number that is more than his chosen number (but less than 10), then ask him to count out that number of objects.

5   Explain to him that the second number is more than the first, for example, "You chose three and then seven, so seven is more than three."

6 Clear away the objects and repeat with different numbers, but this time let him say out loud the phrase "I chose . . . "

7 Once your child is confident in understanding more than, introduce less than; this time start with a number above five and then a number below five.

Also try

Do this activity using dominoes.

Once your child understands this concept with quantities, swap for numerals and use a number line or ruler.

Use other words to describe more than and less than, such as bigger than and smaller than.

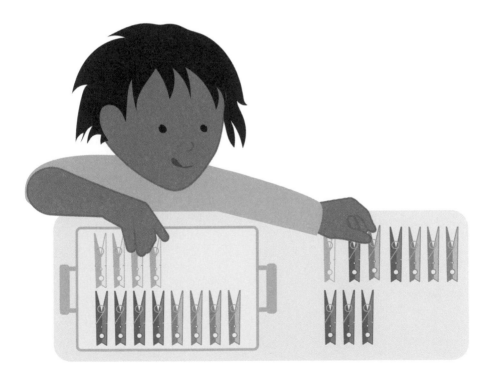

MAKE A PATTERN

Recognizing and constructing a pattern forms an excellent foundation for the development of math skills, such as sequencing, and more complex number operations. This activity can be graded from two matching shapes up to four and can include matching colors.

You will need

- **Paint swatches**
- **Scissors**
- **Sheet of 8.5 x 11 in. paper**
- **Glue stick**
- **Pencil**
- **Ruler**

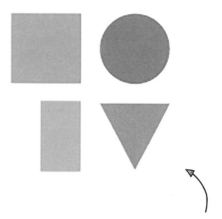

Activity

1   Cut the paint swatches into shapes of circles, squares, rectangles, and triangles.

2   Put the sheet of paper vertically in front of you with the shapes spread out on the left side with the glue stick. Draw a horizontal line of about 7 in. (18 cm) across the top of the page as a guide to where the pattern will go.

3   Invite your child to join you and explain that she is going to make a pattern using two shapes of her choice.

4   Ask her to choose two different shapes and demonstrate where they need to go at the start of the line.

5   Ask her to complete the pattern to the end of the line and then to stick down the shapes.

6   Draw another line below the first. Ask her to choose two different shapes and complete the pattern in the same way, this time without the demonstration. She can go on to complete a third pattern if she wishes. At the end of the activity ask her to describe what she thinks a pattern is.

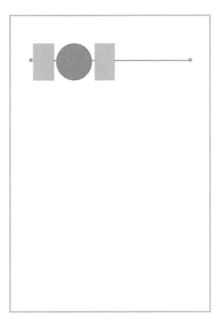

Also try

Make a pattern using three or four contrasting shapes.

Make a pattern using different shapes and colors.

See if your child can spot patterns in your home and outside.

For younger children, use a necklace with different shaped beads to show them what a pattern is.

You can ask your child to help you cut out the shapes.

FIND ME A SHAPE

All children love the game of hide-and-seek; here, shapes are hidden and your child must find them. Starting with basic shapes the activity can be extended to introduce more complex shapes.

You will need

- **4 sheets of colored card or paper**
- **Pencil**
- **Ruler**
- **Scissors**

Activity

1   On the colored pieces of card or paper draw a selection of shapes, such as circles, squares, and rectangles.

2   Cut out the shapes and hide them around the room.

3   Invite your child to find the hidden shapes and bring them to you.

4   When he has found each shape, as him to name it and explain how he can identify it as that shape, for example, he should say, "I have found a triangle. I know it is a triangle because it has three sides."

Also try

Once he is confident in finding circles, squares, and rectangles, introduce shapes with more sides such as pentagons, hexagons, and octagons.

When your child returns with a shape ask him to describe it, "I have found a small blue hexagon, it has six sides."

Encourage your child to look out for shapes in your home and outside.

MAKING PICTURES WITH SHAPES

Teaching children to recognize shapes and their different properties
forms the foundation of their development in both language
and math. Identifying different shapes enables them
to compare, sort, and classify. In addition it helps them
to recognize letters and numerals.

You will need

- 20 paint swatches in different colors
- Scissors
- Sheet of 8.5 x 11 in. paper
- Glue stick
- Ruler

Activity

1   Start by cutting out a selection of shapes from the paint swatches, including circles, triangles, squares, rectangles, diamonds, pentagons, and hexagons.

2   Place the paper on the table, either portrait or landscape, with the shapes and glue stick on the left.

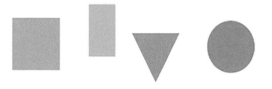

3 Invite your child to see if he can arrange the shapes to make a picture.

4 Let him experiment with the shapes for a while and when he is happy with the arrangement, then he can stick down the pieces.

Also try

When your child is confident with this activity, suggest he makes a picture that includes a pattern, for example petals on a flower.

This activity will help your child when he is constructing puzzles.

Younger children might struggle with ideas, so here are some suggestions: fish, umbrellas in the rain, birds with triangles for feathers, a row of flowers, a house.

MAKING SHAPES

What better way for your child to understand the properties of shapes than by actually making and constructing them. They will learn from making a square that it has four equal sides and from making a triangle that is has three. I have given adaptations for this activity so that it can be done both by children who need help with recognizing their shapes and by those who can confidently identify their shapes.

You will need

- **Toothpicks**
- **Playdough or modeling clay**
- **Tray**

Activity

1 Put the toothpicks and dough onto a tray and ask your child to carry it to a table.

2 Explain to your child that she is going to start by making some 2D shapes, using the sticks and dough to join the pieces.

The end of toothpicks can be sharp, so children need to be reminded to take care and never put sticks near eyes. Younger children will need to be closely supervised when trying this activity.

3 Ask her if she can think of a shape that has three sides and when she replies with "triangle" ask her how many sticks she will need to make the triangle.

4 When she says "three," ask her to take three sticks and arrange them into a triangle on the tray.

5 Now ask her if she can join the triangle using small balls of playdough.

6 Repeat steps 3 to 5, but this time make a square, and then repeat again to make a rectangle.

Also try

Create more complex shapes, like a hexagon or pentagon. Create a 3D shape, like a pyramid.

Write out the names of the shapes individually on large slips of paper. Help your child to read these and place them next to the shapes she has made.

Go on a shape hunt: With the shape names written on large slips of paper, help your child to read the shape name and then see if she can find that shape in the room and place the name on it. For younger children just ask them to find the shape.

NUMBER FANS

Number fans are very easy to make and are a great resource for reinforcing a variety of math concepts, from numeral recognition to sequencing, to more than and less than.

You will need

- **2 sheets of white card measuring 8.5 x 11 in.**
- **Pencil**
- **Scissors**
- **Number line up to 10, or ruler**
- **Black marker**
- **Single hole punch**
- **Keyring**

Activity

1 Copying the illustration on the far right, draw on the card a 4 in. (10 cm) extended teardrop shape. Cut it out and use this as a template to draw nine more fan sections. Cut out all the other fan sections so you have 10 in total.

2 Using the number line as a guide ask your child to write out one number at the widest part of each fan section, starting with zero and finishing with nine.

3 Draw over the numbers with the black marker and punch a single hole into the narrowest part of each fan section.

Ensure the numbers are not written too small; you could do one as an example for size.

4 Attach all the sections using the keyring.

5 Start the game by asking your child to find random numbers. See how quickly he can find that number and hold it up.

6 When he is confident with that, ask him to find two numbers next to each other, and then two numbers farther apart, such as two and four.

Also try

Ask your child to sequence the numbers from zero to five and then from five to nine.

You can ask for numbers more than and less than.

CONSTRUCTING A HOME FOR A TOY

This activity combines elements of mathematics in the comparing of lengths, heights, and volume. There is also an element of design technology in assessing which materials are suitable for the various parts of the home. As far as your child is concerned, she will be having fun making a home for her toy. You'll need an area large enough to construct the home.

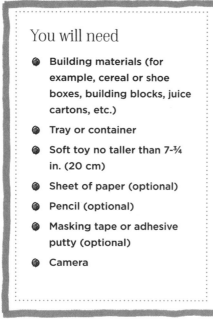

You will need

- **Building materials (for example, cereal or shoe boxes, building blocks, juice cartons, etc.)**
- **Tray or container**
- **Soft toy no taller than 7-¾ in. (20 cm)**
- **Sheet of paper (optional)**
- **Pencil (optional)**
- **Masking tape or adhesive putty (optional)**
- **Camera**

Activity

1 Gather all the building materials and put them onto your tray or container.

2 Ask your child to collect a favorite soft toy.

3 Explain to her that she is going to construct a home for her soft toy and talk about how she would like the home to look: walls, windows, roof, door, etc. If necessary, she could make a drawing of the home.

4 Encourage her to look at the materials and decide which materials will be used for the different parts of the home.

5 Let her construct the home using the materials (and tape if necessary). When complete, put the soft toy inside and take a photo.

Explain that this is her project but that if she needs help she only needs to ask.

Give her plenty of time to think through and explain her ideas.

Also try

Try asking your child to draw the home she would like to build for her toy before starting construction.

Construct other buildings or places that her toy might visit, such as a castle, farm, park, etc.

MEASURING TIME

Do you remember as a child that a week seemed to last forever and the summer vacation an eternity! Children find measuring time very tricky. This activity helps by comparing what different activities can be achieved in one minute. The extension activities continue with this idea but for longer lengths of time.

You will need

- Beads
- String
- Sheet of paper
- Pencil
- Watch (with a second hand)
- Tray

Activity

1   Put the beads, string, paper, pencil, and watch onto the tray and place on the left-hand side of the table.

2   Invite your child to come to the table and explain that he is going to play a game to see what he can do in one minute.

3   Take the watch off the tray and draw his attention to the second hand. Explain that for one minute to pass the second hand will go around the clock face once.

You can swap the activities for those that your child feels confident doing.

For younger children you may wish to start with two-minute challenges.

4 Remove the beads and string from the tray and time him to see how many beads he can thread in one minute.

5 Using the pencil and paper, see how many numbers or letters he can write in one minute.

6 Finally, see how many star jumps he can do in one minute.

Also try

Get your child to observe other lengths of time, for example, use a kitchen timer to see how long it takes to cook some food, or compare how long a certain distance takes when walking and when using another method of transportation.

WHAT'S THE TIME?

When I introduce the concept of time, I talk about how our ancestors would observe the passing of time by the changing seasons and the change from day to night. I also discuss how they would measure time with sundials and sand timers, and finally the need to regulate time to help run our daily life.

You will need

- 2 large paper plates, one just smaller
- Pencil
- Markers
- Ruler
- 8.5 x 11 in. sheet of colored card
- Scissors
- Road head paper fastener
- Glue stick

Activity

1   On the smaller plate ask your child to draw and color a picture or pattern excluding the rim of the plate.

2   Using the ruler and pencil, draw on the card 12 equal-size rectangles, leaving some space at the bottom. Ask your child to write the numbers one to 12 on each rectangle and then cut them out. With the remaining card draw two clock hands and ask him to cut them out.

3   Using your ruler measure equally around the clock face where the numbers need to be placed.

4   Place the smaller plate inside the larger one, mark the point in the center where the clock hands will go, and then cut a hole using the scissors.

Show younger children the numbers on the ruler to help them when they are writing out their numbers for the clock.

5 Place the two clock hands on top of each other and cut a hole through both. Show your child how the paper fastener works and guide him in assembling the clock. Check that the hands move around freely.

6 Ask your child to place and glue down the numbers on the marker points.

7 Start by explaining the hands on the clock: that the longer one counts the minutes and the shorter one the hour. Say to your child, "What time do you get up in the morning?" Show him how to move the clock hands to show that time.

Also try

Use some other times such as the time he goes to school or goes to bed so that he gains confidence in showing the o'clock.

GUESSTIMATE— WITH OBJECTS

The concept of guesstimating is a tricky one for children to grasp, but here it is introduced in a very fun yet concrete way by getting your child to guesstimate the number of marbles needed to fill various containers.

You will need

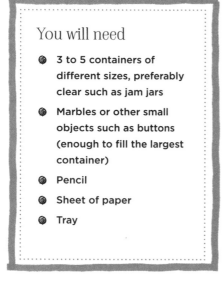

- **3 to 5 containers of different sizes, preferably clear such as jam jars**
- **Marbles or other small objects such as buttons (enough to fill the largest container)**
- **Pencil**
- **Sheet of paper**
- **Tray**

Activity

1   Put your containers, marbles, pencil, and paper on the tray and carry it to the table.

2   Put the containers in a row in the center with the marbles, paper, and pencil to the left.

3   Invite your child to join you and explain that she is going to find out how many marbles it will take to fill each container.

4   Ask her to choose a container and then ask her to guess how many marbles she thinks it would take to fill the container.

5 Now ask her to count marbles into the container and record the answer on the piece of paper.

6 Empty the container of marbles and repeat steps 4 and 5 using another of the containers. Keep repeating until all the containers have been used.

For younger children just use two to three containers.

If your child gets stuck with the guessing part, give them a suggestion, for example "Do you think it will be more than 20?"

Also try

Repeat the activity but this time try filling the containers with smaller or larger objects.

Practice guessing when you are at home or outside, from a stack of plates to the number of items in a shopping cart.

GUESSTIMATE— WITH LIQUIDS

The activity reinforces the concept of guessing but uses liquids rather than objects. Your child will also be called upon to practice his pouring skills as he will be required to pour the water into the container carefully to count how many pitchers are needed to fill it.

You will need

- 3 to 5 clear containers of different sizes, such as jam jars
- Small pitcher
- Large pitcher of water
- Pencil
- Sheet of paper
- Tray

You could add food coloring to help your child see the water line more clearly.

Activity

1   Put the containers, empty pitcher, pitcher of water, pencil, and paper on the tray and carry to the table.

2   Put the containers in a row in the center of the tray with the pitcher and pitcher of water below. Remove the paper and pencil and place to the left of the tray.

3   Invite your child to join you and explain that he is going to find out, first by guessing and then by counting, how many pitchers of water it will take to fill each container.

4   Ask him to choose a container. Remove it from the row and place next to the small pitcher, and then ask him to guess how many pitchers of water he thinks it would take to fill the container.

5 Now, ask him to pour water into the small pitcher and then into the container. Keep repeating until the container is full and record on the piece of paper how many pitchers it took to fill it.

6 Empty the container of water back into the pitcher and repeat steps 4 and 5 using another of the containers. Keep repeating until all the containers have been used.

Also try

Repeat the activity using different size containers and a different size pitcher.

This is a good opportunity to introduce and demonstrate the terms full, empty, half, and a quarter. Ask your child to pour colored water into a clear container marked with levels for full, half full, etc.

COMBINING QUANTITIES AND NUMERALS

Using the number rods and number cards together helps to combine your child's understanding of quantity with the numerals 1 to 10. The number rods act as a visual tool that can be counted to establish a relationship between the figures on the cards and the quantities they represent.

You will need

- **Number cards from pages 100–101**
- **Number rods (Worksheet 5, and see pages 94–95)**
- **Tray**

2   Ask your child, "Can you find rod 4?" Your child will need to count the rods until she finds the correct rod.

3   Now say, "Can you find how we write four?" When your child finds the "4" card, ask her to place it at the end of rod 4.

4   Choose another number, and follow the same steps. Continue until all the number cards have been placed next to their matching quantity (rod).

Activity

1   Put the cards and rods onto the tray and ask your child to carry it to the table. Place the number rods horizontally in front of your child in any order. Place the number cards to the right in any order.

Take this opportunity to introduce other ways of asking for a number. This helps with language and mathematical skills. For example, use "Find me . . ." or "What is this . . . ?"

Also try

When you see that your child can match the rods and cards, show her how to build the rods and cards into numerical order. Start with the rods, and build a staircase shape by lining up the rods from shortest to longest. When this is complete, show your child how to match the cards with the rods, showing 1 and 2 only. Invite her to complete the matching.

BUILD A SERIES OF NUMBERS

Building a series of numbers reinforces counting and matching the correct quantity to the relevant numeral. The placement of the counters below the cards also introduces the concept of odd and even numbers.

You will need

- Number cards from pages 100–101
- 55 counters, buttons, beads, or coins
- Container to hold counters
- Number rods from previous activity
- Ruler

Activity

1   Ask your child to take the container with the counters to the table. You take the number cards. Ask your child to sit with the containers in front of her. Mix the cards, and place them above the container to your child's right.

2   Ask your child to find the number one, and to place the card on her left above the container. Then ask how many counters she will need to place under it. Ask her to place the counter under the number.

3   Ask your child what comes after one. Encourage her to find the number "2" card, and then two counters to place underneath, side-by-side.

4 Follow the steps for numbers "3" or "4," then ask your child to continue to number 10 by herself. Give her some guidance on the placement of the counters; the "even" number counters need to be in two columns next to each other, while the "odd" number counters need to have the extra counter placed on the left-hand column.

5 If your child makes a mistake with the sequence of numbers, wait until she has completed the activity, then ask her to compare her numbers with the ruler.

Also try

When your child can work independently at this activity, point to the counters and ask if she notices any similarity about them. Explain that numbers that can be put into pairs like two, four, and six are known as "even" numbers. Also explain that numbers without a pair like one, three, and five are known as "odd" numbers.

To reinforce odd and even numbers, set out four small objects in the same pattern as the counters. Ask your child to count the objects. Ask if the three or four is an odd or even number. If she is not sure, remind her about the rule of even numbers always having a "partner" while odd numbers always have one left over.

MAKING LADYBUGS FOR MATH ACTIVITIES

Children love insects and in particular they are drawn to ladybugs with their distinctive color markings. Here, your child will make ladybugs with the numbers one to 10, which can be used for a variety of math activities.

You will need

- 10 small sheets of white card
- Pencil
- Picture of a ladybug
- Paintbrush
- Red poster paint
- Ruler
- Coin
- Black marker

Activity

1   Start by drawing the shape of a ladybug on each piece of card.

2   Explain to your child that he will be making ladybugs and invite him to paint all the ladybugs red. Allow to dry.

3   Using the ruler draw a pencil line down the center of each ladybug body and mark off the head and bottom end.

4   Make spots by drawing around the coin, adding the number of spots for each of the numbers one to 10; for the even numbers make pairs of spots on either side of the center line and for odd numbers make pairs with one left over at the bottom.

Also try

You can use the ladybugs for sequencing and counting activities: You can match numerals to the spots and they can be used for many additional activities.

Make a set of ladybugs with numbers up to 20 (in this case use larger pieces of card).

Draw teddy bears instead of ladybugs, with buttons instead of spots.

5 Ask your child to color in the spots, head, and bottom end using the marker. Using your ruler, draw over the center line with the pen.

6 Draw the legs in pencil and ask your child to go over them using the marker.

Ensure you use all the space on the card for your ladybug.

Check that the coin you use is small enough to fit all 10 spots on the last ladybug.

You could make a template of a ladybug to draw around.

ODD AND EVEN NUMBERS

In this classic Montessori activity, your child will learn to spot the difference between odd and even numbers by seeing that even numbers always come in pairs while odd numbers have one left over. This activity uses the cards from Making Ladybugs for Math Activities, but if you have not made these then instead use counters or coins.

You will need

- **Set of ladybug cards (see page 132)**
- **55 counters or coins**

For younger children just start with the numbers one to five.

If your child is having difficulty recognizing the pattern, then use your finger to point out the odd spot with no partner.

Activity

1   Place the ladybug cards in the middle of the table.

2   Invite your child to come to the table and explain that she is going to explore odd and even numbers.

3   Ask her to set out the ladybug cards from left to right in the correct sequence.

4   Starting with number one, ask her to place a counter over the spot. Repeat with the remaining cards.

5   Ask her to compare the pattern of spots, for example, between five and six and between nine and 10. She should observe that on the six and 10 cards all the dots have partners while on the five and nine cards have one dot without a partner.

6   Explain to her that two, four, six, eight, and 10 are known as even numbers because they come in pairs, while one, three, five, seven, and nine are called odd numbers because they always have one left over.

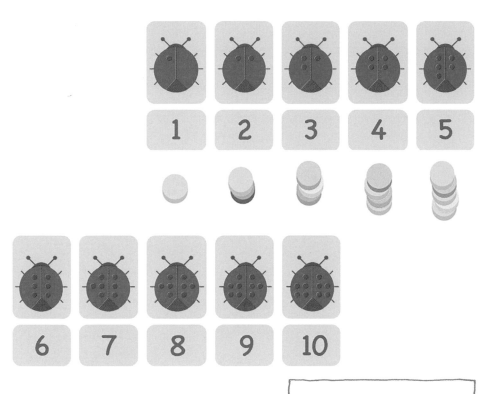

Also try

Write out the words "odd" and "even" and place under the relevant ladybugs.

Your child can place the numerals under the ladybugs with the correct quantity of spots.

Look at a set of dominoes or dice with your child and see if she can work out which are odd and which are even.

CUPS AND COUNTERS

Counting with cups and counters is another visual way to reinforce the numerals with their corresponding quantity. The inclusion of one empty container also focuses on the concept of zero (0).

You will need

- 45 counters, buttons, beads, or coins
- 10 cups or small containers
- Strip of paper about 20 in. (50 cm) long
- Black marker
- Shallow container to hold counters

Write the numerals 0 to 9 across the strip of paper, spaced evenly. Put the counters into the container and place everything onto a tray.

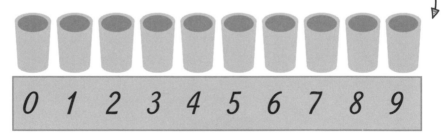

0 1 2 3 4 5 6 7 8 9

Activity

1. Ask your child to carry the tray to the table and to sit where he can see clearly. Place the container with the counters in front of him and the number strip behind it, and place the cups in a row behind the paper strip.

2. Point to the number strip and ask your child to read the numbers on it. Return to the "0" and say that it is called "zero." Explain that it means "nothing" so he will be putting no counters in that cup.

3. Point to the "1" and ask your child to put that number of counters in the cup above.

4. Point to the "2," and repeat the same instructions. Repeat for "3" and "4." Continue to "9" if your child would like to.

5. If you notice that he has put an incorrect number of counters into a cup, do not be tempted to correct at this point. When he has completed the activity, say, "Let's check that we have got the right number of counters in the cups." When you are counting together, allow him to discover that he has made an error in his counting.

Also try

Return to the "Objects on a line" activity on pages 98–99. Take another bag to match the others, and place it before the "1" bag on the line. Explain to your child that it represents zero. Ask him if he can remember what zero means. He should reply "nothing." Then ask if he will need to put anything in the bag. If he has any difficulty remembering, you can give him hints, such as reminding him that it comes before one.

The activity uses 45 counters, which is exactly what your child will need to be able to count up to nine. If he has too few or too many at the end, it will be a clue to check the cups.

ADDING NUMERALS TO OBJECTS

Now that your child has learned both the quantities and numerals from 0 to 10, you can add the numerals to the "Objects on a line" already created (see pages 98–99).

You will need

- Number cards from pages 100–101
- Black marker
- Colored pens or pencils

Draw around each number using the pen, to create large numerals with space for your child to color in.

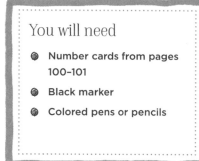

Activity

1   Ask your child to color in the numerals. When she has finished, explain that the numbers are going to be put up on the "Objects on a line" you made before.

2   Lay out the number cards under the object number line in a random order. Point to the first bag and ask your child if there is anything in the bag. She should respond with "yes." You respond with, "Which number is the same as the number of items in the bag?" Point to the numerals on the floor and she should pick out the "1." Help her to attach it to the first bag.

3   Point to the bag with one object in and ask her, "How many objects are in this bag?" Ask her to find the number "1" and help her to add it to the line. Continue these steps until you reach "10."

Also try

Make cardboard ladybugs (see page 134), without their spots. Involve your child with coloring the ladybugs, and work with her to add the spots, from 0 to 10. When complete, hang them on the line across the room. This is a time-consuming and enjoyable activity, so you might like to spread it over a week.

If your child can't remember the next number quantity, take the bag off the line and ask her to count the objects.

ADDITION UP TO 10

Now that your child has learned the quantities and numerals from 0 to 10, you can introduce her to addition. This activity follows the same pattern as the other number activities, in that it begins adding in quantity only, and later introduces the numerals and signs required.

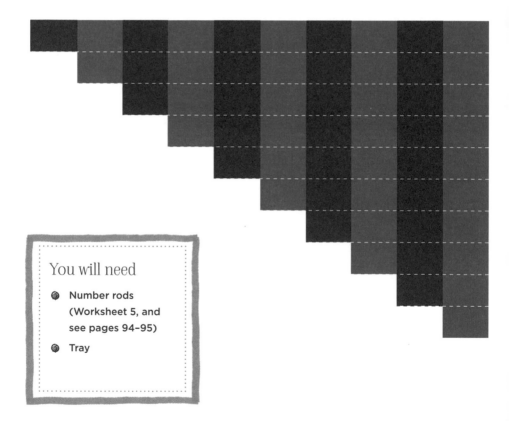

You will need

- Number rods (Worksheet 5, and see pages 94–95)
- Tray

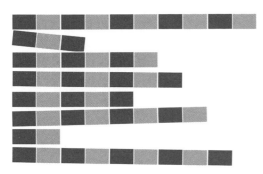

Activity

1. Ask your child to carry the tray with the number rods to the table. Put the number rods in a random order in front of her. Ask her to build the number rods into a stair.

2. Say, "I am going to show you how to do addition using the number rods." Ask your child to find the rod 1, and to place it below the stair. Then ask her to find number rod 4 and put it next to rod 1. Select numbers under five, to keep it easy.

3. Ask her to count along the joined rods to see what number she gets. Make sure that your child uses a finger to count carefully each number rod section. When she gives the answer "five," explain that, "One plus four equals five." As you are saying this, point to the individual number rods.

4. Ask your child to put back the rods, and then do several more addition sums. Remember to use low numbers.

5. When your child understands the objective of the activity, tell her that she can make up her own sum. Ask her to choose two numbers, then ask her to tell you the sum. For example, "Five plus three equals . . . " You may need to explain the words "plus" and "equals" to her.

6. When she has finished the activity, review the steps that got her to her answer. Remind her that the number she finishes with must always be bigger than the two numbers that she started with.

ADDITION USING NUMERALS

When your child has mastered the concept of addition with quantities (using number rods), you can introduce numerals using the number cards from previous activities to construct a sum. As your child progresses, introduce sums written on paper (see "Also try").

You will need

- Number cards (see page 100)
- Number rods (Worksheet 5)
- Card
- Black marker

Draw an equals sign (=) and a plus sign (+) on the card and cut out to the same size as your number cards.

Activity

1   Lay out the number cards and number rods in order. Ask your child to choose a number rod and place it on the table in front of him.

2   Ask your child to find the matching number card, and place it under the number rod. Place the "+" card next to the selected number card, and explain that it means "plus."

3   Ask your child to select another number rod and card, and place them after the plus sign. Place the "=" card after the second number, and explain that it is the sign for "equals."

4 Ask your child what he needs to do next, and he should tell you, "Count the numbers," or "Add them together." Help him to reach the answer using the number rods to count, if necessary.

5 When he reaches the answer, put it next to the equals sign. Do several more sums with your child until he is ready to make up his own sums.

Also try

When your child is confident with the number cards, introduce working sums written on paper. He may also eventually like to write his own sums.

SUBTRACTION UNDER 10

Generally, children find the concept of subtraction easier to grasp than addition. For example, they often understand that if you have six apples and give three away, there are three apples left. You might like to try this activity before the previous one. Because your child will already be familiar with recording addition sums, both the quantity and the numerals are introduced at the same time in this activity.

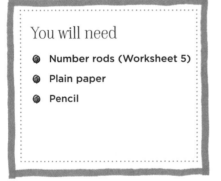

You will need

- **Number rods (Worksheet 5)**
- **Plain paper**
- **Pencil**

Activity

1   Ask your child to carry the number rods to the table and to sit on your left. Ask her to build the number rods into a stair, leaving a space below.

2   Take out two rods and place them together. Ask your child to count the sections and discover the total. Remove the lowest number rod, and ask your child to count what is left. Do two more sums in this way, so that your child begins to see the processes involved.

3   When the fourth sum has been completed, repeat the steps but add questions such as, "We started with how many?," "Then we took away how many?," and "We were left with how

many?" Finish by summarizing. For example, "So five take away three leaves two."

4   Show your child how to record the sum on paper, explaining that this is how we write this sum. Do two more sums in this way, with you doing the recording for your child.

5   When your child is ready to record the sum, ask her to do it as she goes through the steps. Otherwise, she will forget the number that she started with, and the number she "took away."

Also try

Show your child addition and subtraction in everyday situations. For example, demonstrate with fruit, blocks, toys, etc.

NUMBER SONGS AND RHYMES

These are an excellent way to reinforce numbers and number concepts because of the rhyming element and the actions, which act as a memory aid. They can be taught to children of any age.

Once I Caught A Fish Alive

This song reinforces the number sequence, and counting in ones. Count out the numbers on your fingers as you say them.

One, two, three, four, five,

Once I caught a fish alive.

Six, seven, eight, nine, ten;

Then I let him go again.

Why did you let him go?

Because he bit my finger so.

Which finger did he bite?

This little finger on my right.

One, Two, Buckle My Shoe

This song also counts in numerical order. You could count out the numbers on your fingers, and do some of the actions.

One, two, buckle my shoe,

Three, four, knock at the door,

Five, six, pick up sticks,

Seven, eight, lay them straight,

Nine, ten, a big fat hen.

There Were Ten in the Bed

Children really enjoy acting out this song by lying on a bed or standing. Each verse, one child will fall down to the floor. The song can start with the number of children playing.

There were ten in the bed

And the little one said,

"Roll over! Roll over!"

So they all rolled over and

One fell out,

There were nine in the bed

And the little one said,

"Roll over! Roll over!"

So they all rolled over and

One fell out, etc.

Ten Fat Sausages

This song is a firm favorite with the children I teach. It also involves subtraction, and counting down in twos. When you get to "pop," make a pop sound with your index finger inside your mouth. Clap your hands together for "bang."

Ten fat sausages sizzling in a pan,

One went pop and the other went bang.

Eight fat sausages sizzling in a pan,

One went pop and the other went bang.

Six fat sausages sizzling in a pan, etc.

Ten Green Bottles

You could use plastic bottles to follow the actions, or you could change the words to use teddy bears or other suitable objects.

Ten green bottles hanging on a wall,

Ten green bottles hanging on a wall,

And if one green bottle should accidentally fall,

There'll be nine green bottles hanging on the wall.

PIZZA PLAY

All young children love pizza and playing with dough. This activity combines the two. By creating their own pizza parlor they have a framework in which to exercise their imaginative and role-playing ideas. This is best done with several children.

You will need

- Playdough
- 1 sheet of 8.5 x 11 in. paper per child, plus 4 extra sheets
- Colored markers
- Old pizza boxes
- Glue stick
- 2 protective cloths for work and parlor areas
- Apron per child
- If possible, a child-size rolling pin for each child (if you don't have any rolling pins, use something like a plastic cup)
- Plastic knives
- Paper plates

Activity

1   Start by preparing the dough for creating the pizzas. (You may want to use different colors of dough for the pizza dough and the toppings.)

2   Explain to the children that they are going to make their own pizza parlor.

PIZZA MENU

MARGHERITA
HAWAIIAN
PEPPERONI
FOUR CHEESE

After the activity, check the bottom of your children's shoes. Dough sticks very easily to the soles.

Remind your children that this dough is definitely not for eating.

3 Write out a sign and labels for the parlor. Stick the labels onto the boxes and put the sign in the work area.

4 Write out a menu offering four varieties of pizza on a piece of paper. Tell the children what the choices are.

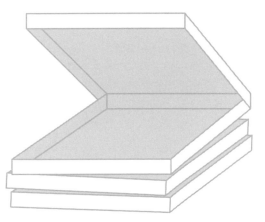

5 Put a protective tablecloth on the work area. Ask the children to put on their aprons and help you set out the dough and the tools.

6 On another table put out the other protective tablecloth and ask the children to help count out the correct number of paper plates for the customers.

7 If there are several children, divide them into two groups—the pizza makers and the customers. (They can trade places after a while.) Otherwise, prevail upon any available adults to be customers.

8 Ask the pizza makers to first take orders from the customers. Help them to make a mark on the pizza menu next to the pizza selected, so you can count together how many pizzas are needed.

9 Ask the children to make their pizza and, when finished, put the pizzas into the boxes and give them to the customers.

10 When everyone has had an opportunity to make some pizza, close the pizza parlor and ask everyone to help clear up. The dough can be stored back in the bags and kept in the refrigerator to use again.

Also try

Once your child has played this, you may like to vary the game by changing the setting. Instead of a pizza parlor, it could be a bakery, and your child could make little cupcakes for all of her customers.

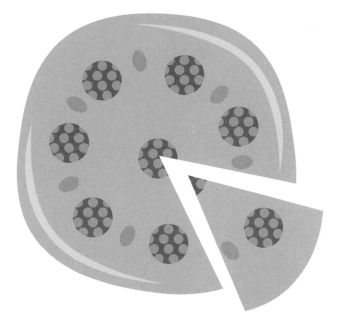

DICE ADDITION

Dice, the bigger the better, are an invaluable resource for a variety of math activities. I recommend introducing this activity alongside "Introducing Numbers Beyond 10" (see page 96–97), as the sums can reach up to 12. As usual, this activity starts with using just the quantities and then extends to introducing the plus and minus signs along with number cards.

You will need

- Pair of dice (as big as you can find)
- Number cards up to 12
- Tray
- 1 plus and 1 equal sign, each written on a small piece of card or paper

Activity

1   Put the dice and the cards onto the tray and ask your child to take it to your chosen work area. (I normally introduce this activity on the floor.) Ask her to remove the dice from the tray and place in the center of the work area.

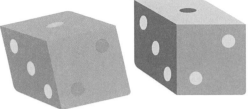

2 With your child sitting on your left explain to her that she is going to use the dice to make additions.

3 Roll one die and then the other, count out loud the dots on both dice to make the total. Pointing to each die in turn explain how you did this, for example, "I rolled a four, then a two and added them together to make six."

4 Hand the dice to her and invite her to try. Repeat at least three times until she is confident with the activity.

5 Introduce the plus and equal signs and say that you are going to put them into your addition. Repeat step 3 but instead say "four plus," insert the plus sign "two equals," insert the equals sign "six," put down the six number card.

6 Invite her to try using the plus and minus sign and number cards. Repeat at least twice more until she is sure of the steps of the game.

Also try

Once your child is confident with this activity, she can try recording the sum on a whiteboard or paper.

For younger children you may wish to just do steps 1 to 4 and leave steps 5 to 6 for another time.

DOUBLE IT

Knowing how to double a number is excellent preparation for when your child goes on to learn multiplication. This activity starts by doubling two using quantities of objects and can be extended to using numerals.

You will need

- 30 small counters, such as buttons or beads
- Container

Activity

1   Put the counters in the container and place on the left-hand side of the table.

2   Invite your child to come and play Double It.

3   Ask your child to put two counters on the table in a horizontal line on the left.

4   Tell him that you both are now going to double the number two.

For younger children just go up to six to start with, and then work up to 10.

Leave spaces between the counters so that your child can clearly see the quantities for each of the numbers.

5 Ask him to put two counters in a horizontal line on the right, and then add two more underneath to form a square. Ask him to count the counters and say "four."

6 Repeat steps 4 and 5, adding an extra two counters each time, until you reach 10. Review the game and ask him to say out loud "two," "four," "six," "eight," "10" while pointing to the correct groups of counters.

Also try

Once your child is confident with the quantities, add numerals under each quantity of counters and say out loud the operation, for example, "We had two and added two more to make four," then ask your child to select the correct numeral and place under the four counters.

You can try counting in threes.

Once your child is confident up to 10, try going higher.

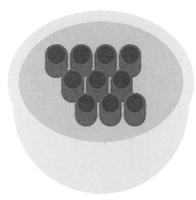

MEASURING WITH NONSTANDARD UNITS

This is an excellent activity for children to understand the concept of measuring as they will be using their hands to measure objects. I always introduce this activity with a discussion about what people used when there were no rulers. You could mention that the heights of ponies and horses are still measured in hands. By the end of this activity your child should come to understand why we converted to standard units of measuring.

You will need

- Sheet of paper
- Pencil
- 6 to 8 medium to large objects, such as table top, chair, book, kitchen cabinet, sink, etc.

Activity

1   Invite your child to come and join you and explain that he is going to do some measuring. Explain that he is not going to use a ruler but instead a part of his body. Ask him to guess which part.

2   On the paper write down the objects to be measured in a column on the left. He can help you with this.

3   Demonstrate to him how to measure so that there are no gaps between the fingertips and the base of the other hand.

For younger children start with just four to six objects

Also try

Measure objects using your feet.

4   Measure the first object yourself and, before he
    measures it himself, ask if he thinks the number of
    his hands needed will be higher or lower than yours.
    Ask him to measure the object to see if he is correct.

5   Record on the paper the number of hands measured
    for the first object.

6   Let him continue measuring and recording the rest
    of the objects.

68

MATH OPPOSITES— LARGE AND SMALL

Alongside your child's development in understanding math concepts comes a development in math vocabulary. This is particularly the case in describing math opposites. Over the next pages there are three activities exploring math opposites. We start with comparing larger and smaller objects.

You will need

- 4 to 5 small objects (such as buttons, a pencil, a coin, etc.)
- 4 to 5 large objects (such as jars, bottles, cans, etc.)
- Tray

Activity

1 Place all the objects on the tray and carry to the table. Place the tray on the left side of the table.

2 Invite your child to come and join you and tell her she is going to investigate large and small by comparing the objects.

3 Ask her to put all the objects in a row at the top in any order.

4 Explain to her that the objective is to pair one large and one small object. Demonstrate by choosing a large object and a small one and place them in the center just below the row of objects side by side with the larger on the left.

5 Let her continue the activity by selecting another pair, reminding her to place the larger object on the left and smaller on the right.

6 Continue until all the objects have been paired.

Also try

Compare three objects, large, larger, largest and small, smaller, smallest.

Grade the objects in size from the largest to the smallest.

For younger children, start with just three of each size.

Make sure that there is a big difference in size between the objects.

69

MATH OPPOSITES— LONG AND SHORT

In everyday life we are often asked to compare length; this activity teaches your child how to do this by finding hidden pieces of string and comparing them with his piece, which will act as a comparison marker. Once your child feels confident in this activity he can go on to grading the strings from longest to shortest and then be introduced to using a ruler.

You will need

- Ball of string or yarn
- Scissors
- Ruler
- Masking tape or adhesive putty (optional)

Activity

1 Cut a 12 in. (30 cm) piece of string, then cut four pieces longer and four shorter.

2 Hide the eight longer and shorter pieces of string around the room, some of which could be stretched out and taped to a surface like a wall or shelf.

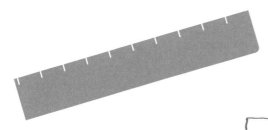

3   Invite your child to come and find
    the pieces of string hidden around
    the room.

4   Give him the 12 in. (30 cm) piece
    of string to use as a measure of
    comparison. When he finds a piece of
    string he needs to compare whether it
    is longer or shorter than his piece.

Also try

Grade the strings: When your child
has found them all, he should bring
them to the table and put them in
order from longest to shortest.

This activity is an excellent
introduction to using a ruler and
when your child is confident, do
this activity using a ruler.

Using your child's piece of
string and an extra piece that
is shorter or longer, show him
how to correctly compare
lengths by ensuring both
ends of the string are lined up
equally on one side.

MATH OPPOSITES— HEAVY AND LIGHT

When we compare lengths, we can trust our eyes to judge correctly, but the same doesn't apply to comparing weights. In this activity your child will discover that, generally, it is the materials that an object is made from and not the size that determines its weight.

You will need

- **6 to 8 objects of different sizes and weights**
- **Tray**

Activity

1   Place the objects on the tray in pairs of contrasting weights and place the tray on the left-hand side of the table.

2   Invite your child to come and join you to see if she can work out which is the heavier of each pair of objects.

3   Invite her to select the first pair of objects and ask her which she thinks is the heavier of the two.

4   Repeat with the other pairs.

5   Repeat the activity, but this time allow her to hold the objects one in each hand to compare the weights.

6   She should discover that weight is not always based on size but also on the materials the object is made from.

Also try

Grade the objects from heaviest to lightest.

This activity opens up a whole new investigation of which materials are heavier and lighter and best suited to certain types of jobs. The perfect story to investigate this is *The Three Little Pigs*.

For younger children just do steps 1–4 and then progress on to steps 5–6.

Choose objects that are big in size but light in weight and vice versa.

WRAPPING A PRESENT

Every child loves receiving a present and I find they equally like the challenge of wrapping one. This activity combines several math skills, starting with learning to judge the correct size of paper to wrap the object and extending to learning to cut the correct size of paper.

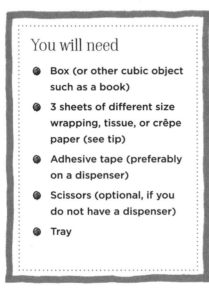

You will need

- Box (or other cubic object such as a book)
- 3 sheets of different size wrapping, tissue, or crêpe paper (see tip)
- Adhesive tape (preferably on a dispenser)
- Scissors (optional, if you do not have a dispenser)
- Tray

Activity

1   Place all the items onto the tray and ask your child to carry them to the floor or table.

2   Place the box in the center of the work space with the three pieces of paper in a row above and the other items to the left of where your child will be sitting.

3   Explain to your child that the challenge is for him to wrap the box and select the paper that will best cover and fit the box.

4   Ask him to try testing the papers to see which he thinks will fit best.

5   When he has selected the sheet that best fits, demonstrate to him how to center the box and wrap the paper around, slightly overlapping. Explain that he will need to tape it down and then let him try.

6   Move on to the ends, demonstrating how to fold each side into a triangle, bend up the end and attach with tape. Guide him through how to do the other end.

Also try

Wrap different shaped objects.

When your child is confident with this activity, progress to using a roll of paper. For this activity the paper rolls with a marked grid on the back are really helpful as a cutting guide.

Demonstrate how to wrap ribbon around the object, then build up to adding a bow.

For younger children have just two sheets of paper to choose from.

For the three sheets of paper make one the correct size, one too small, and the other too big.

WORKSHEET 1

The phonic alphabet
Letters of the alphabet with their phonic sounds.

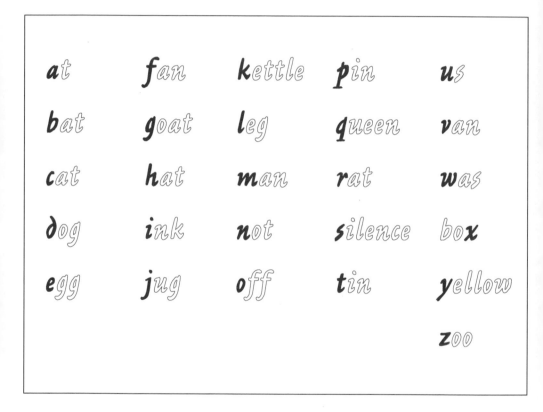

at	fan	kettle	pin	us
bat	goat	leg	queen	van
cat	hat	man	rat	was
dog	ink	not	silence	box
egg	jug	off	tin	yellow
				zoo

WORKSHEET 2

Identifying letters

Cut out each letter along the dotted lines.

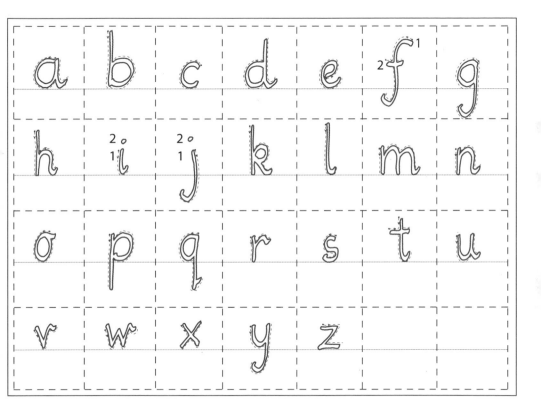

WORKSHEET 3

Word building

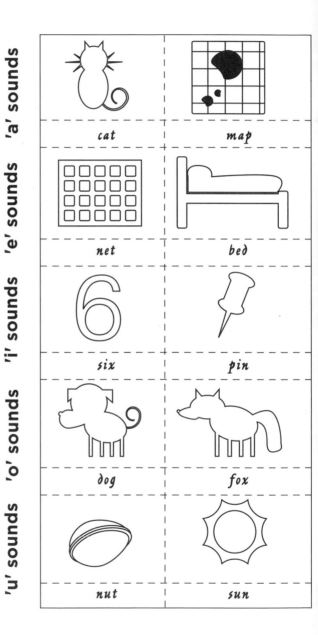

'a' sounds

cat   map

'e' sounds

net   bed

'i' sounds

six   pin

'o' sounds

dog   fox

'u' sounds

nut   sun

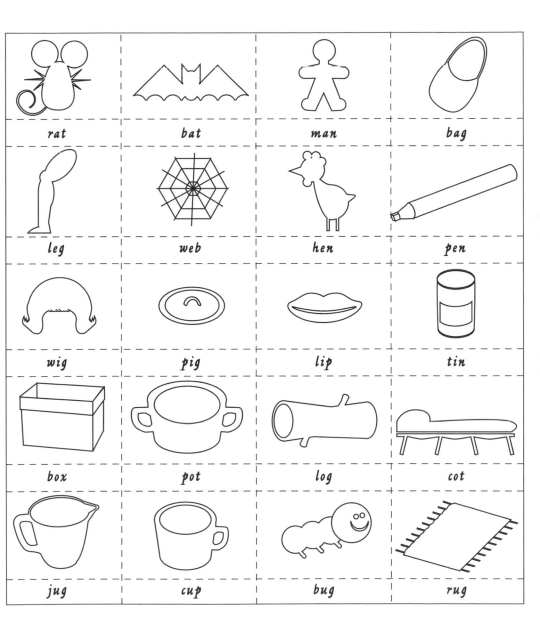

rat	*bat*	*man*	*bag*
leg	*web*	*hen*	*pen*
wig	*pig*	*lip*	*tin*
box	*pot*	*log*	*cot*
jug	*cup*	*bug*	*rug*

WORKSHEET 4

Constructing phrases

Article	Adjective	Verb	Preposition
The	big	sat	on
A	red	jumps	under
the	pink	hops	over
a	wet	digs	next to
	little	runs	by

up		
put	looks	saw
goes	creeps	rolls
hot	slim	thin
soft	spotted	stripy

WORKSHEET 5

Learning height and length Cut out each rod along the dotted lines.

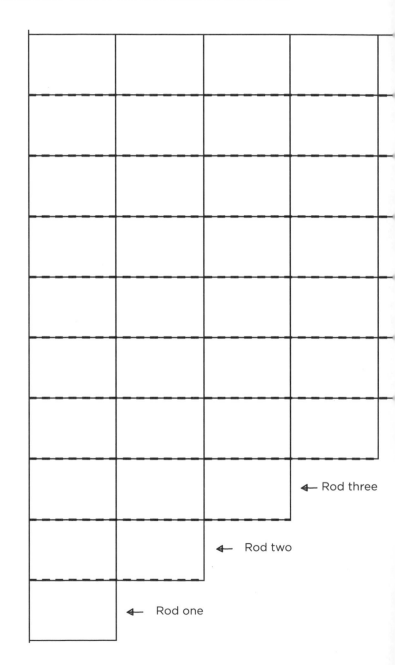

← Rod three

← Rod two

← Rod one

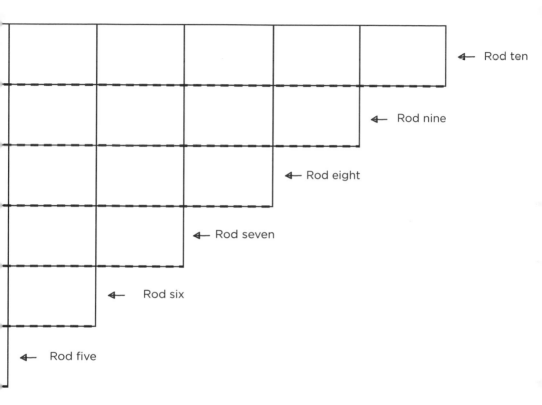

← Rod ten

← Rod nine

← Rod eight

← Rod seven

← Rod six

← Rod five

r

WORKSHEET 6

Story gloves

Cut out the figures to tell the story
of *Goldilocks and the Three Bears*